PRAISE FOR
DAWN WARRIOR

Vulnerable, heartfelt and inspiring, *Dawn Warrior* is the book every mother needs to read. Tara's beautiful and authentic real-life story is perfectly intertwined with practical advice to help you unlock a life of happiness and balance – all achieved by embracing the Dawn Warrior mindset. Creating the time all mothers deserve is the secret to self-love, and this overflows into the lives of our children and creates positive ripples across the world.

Clare Wood
Business coach & money mentor
clarewood.com

Dawn Warrior is a wonderful read and an important reminder of how to stay on course and in flow while honouring our roles as mothers. Tara has written a book that is not only inspirational but practical.

Bernadette Somers
Intuitive mentor, physiotherapist & author of *Yolk*
bernadettesomers.com

Packed with tools and mindset hacks, this inspiring and motivating read will help every mum to reconnect to her soul's purpose and find inner peace. Tara openly and powerfully shares her journey of overcoming depression, infertility and eating disorders, and shows you how you, too, can set yourself free from limiting beliefs, unleash your power and create a life on *your* terms. If you are a mum who wants to learn the secrets to creating more energy and joy, this book is for you.

Madelaine Vallin
Founder of Australian School of Holistic Counselling
madelainevallin.com

Tara is a total inspiration, and her book *Dawn Warrior* is a life-changer. She captures the mix of delight and wonder, as well as challenge and overwhelm, that can happen to all women during the seismic shift that is motherhood. This book is a much-needed warm hug for any woman who is undergoing this unique personal journey.

Dahlas Fletcher
Mother of three, pregnancy and postpartum exercise specialist & founder of BodyFabulous Fitness
bodyfabulous.com.au

This beautiful book will hold, support and guide you as you lean into the magic of the morning and discover the power, peace and potential of the Dawn Warrior within you.

Sarah Jensen
Heart healer & journaling expert
sarahjensen.com.au

Enlightening, thought-provoking and inspiring – this delightful work by Tara is a beautiful read. She shows it is possible, as a new mother, to increase energy and navigate motherhood with calmness and clarity, all while getting in touch with your purpose. The risk of losing yourself at this transformative time is very real. However, Tara shows how you can make a choice and take action to avoid this happening to you. Thank you, Tara, for sharing your wisdom and strategies and paving the way for other mamas.

Cheryl Sheriff
Mother, doula, midwife & author of *Stork Talk: Delivering strategies for your ideal birth*
idealbirth.com.au

DAWN WARRIOR

THE MODERN MAMA'S GUIDE
TO HARNESSING YOUR POWER AND CREATING A LIFE YOU LOVE

TARA HEGERTY

First published in 2021 by Tara Hegerty
dawnwarrior.com

© Tara Hegerty 2021

The moral rights of the author have been asserted.

All rights reserved. Except as permitted under international copyright laws, no part of this book may be reproduced in any form or by any means, be stored in a retrieval system, or be communicated or transmitted in any form or by any means, without prior written permission. All enquiries should be made to the publisher at the above website.

Publishing consultancy: Rich Life by Design | richlifebydesign.com
Cover design: Amy De Wolfe | amydewolfe.com
Interior design and layout: Amy De Wolfe | amydewolfe.com
Cover photo: Jared Lank | jaredlank.com
Back-cover author photo: Lindy Yewen | lindyphotography.com.au
Photo on page 195: Lindy Yewen | lindyphotography.com.au

A catalogue record for this work is available from the National Library of Australia

ISBN: 9780645110807

Disclaimer

The author of this book does not dispense medical, psychological, financial, legal or business advice or prescribe the use of any technique as a form of treatment for associated problems without the advice of a relevant professional, either directly or indirectly. The intent of the author is only to offer information of a general nature to help you improve your life. In the event that you use the information in this book for yourself, the author assumes no responsibility for your actions. The views, thoughts and opinions expressed within this book belong solely to the author.

Dedication

This book is dedicated to you, Mama. May your life shine, one morning at a time.

CONTENTS

A Message from Tara 11
A Gift for You 15
Introduction 17

Part 1: The Dawn & the Warrior

Chapter 1: A Deeper Dive Into My Story 27
Chapter 2: The Four Elements 37
Chapter 3: Awaken Your Inner Voice 45
Chapter 4: The Law of Attraction 51
Chapter 5: What Lights You Up? 59

Part 2: Design Your Life with the Five Ps

Chapter 6: The Three Questions 71
Chapter 7: P1 – Physical 77
Chapter 8: P2 – Psychological 87
Chapter 9: P3 – Partnerships 97
Chapter 10: P4 – Parenting 111
Chapter 11: P5 – Professional 121

Part 3: Becoming Who You Are

Chapter 12: Bringing Your Purpose into Being 139
Chapter 13: Embrace Your Mornings 145
Chapter 14: The Golden Hour 153
Chapter 15: On Loving Yourself 163

Chapter 16: Living Your Vision 171
Chapter 17: The Dawn Warrior Way: A Summary 181

In Memoriam 185
Thanks 189
About Tara 193
The Dawn Warrior Way 195

A MESSAGE FROM TARA

Hi Mama

This book is a collection of lessons and practices that have pushed me to a place of self-compassion and resilience – the place of a true warrior. My approach is birthed from perseverance and the discovery of self-advocacy. It's rooted in owning my truth in a way that is honest to the woman I am today.

Every day, I find within myself the strength to win the battles that show up in my life as a mama. The greatest lesson my warrior journey has taught me is that there are always more challenges, and more joy to expand into. Unfolding never stops. And, to be honest, I wish someone had told my younger self that there is no finish line. But just like the sun dawning anew, I begin again. Often it isn't until we sit with our unique experiences, over time, that we are given the gift of glory.

As you travel your own path, may this book give you hope and may this message settle into your heart: you are here to rise. Here's to uncovering your Dawn Warrior and believing that you deserve to be an empowered mama, one morning at a time.

Here are a few things you need to know before we get started:

It works!

The Dawn Warrior system is tried and true. It has been tested by me but also by other modern mamas. I share tools, techniques and exercises throughout the book. I want you to engage with the book, take notes, write in the margins and make it your own.

My mantras for inspiration

In a few special chapters I've included my personal mantras. I hope that they inspire you, and please feel free to create your own.

Golden Hour Affirmations

These affirmations are here to nudge you back onto your life path. You'll see these popping up throughout this book, and they are designed to be short, sweet and powerful. I encourage you to really embrace their wisdom by taking a photo of them or writing them down, sticking them on your bathroom mirror or using them as inspiration to create your own. Their simple, intuitive wisdom is seriously potent.

Are you a research nerd, like me?

For mamas who want a deeper dive into the concepts of this book, I've created a resource list that outlines all of the sources I used in its creation, along with suggestions for further reading. It is a PDF with clickable links, which makes it easy to access everything. You can download this PDF here: dawnwarrior.com/bookresources.

The Dawn Warrior Way

The system in this book is how I actually live my life. I walk my talk: Every. Single. Morning. My mission is to support and inspire you by providing personalised guidance and real time accountability, and this is why I have created *The Dawn Warrior Way* online program. It includes heaps of extra resources, including worksheets, and habit and goal trackers, and it features valuable personal guidance from your very own mama mentor (me!). It is also the hub for a community of co-elevating women who live consciously, and who make the world a better place by first making their own lives better. If all of this sounds like a dream come true, head to dawnwarrior.com/dawnwarriorway to discover more.

Connect with me

I love connecting with my readers. You'll find me on Instagram (@dawnwarrior), where I share new stories and ideas — I would love to connect with you on that platform. To learn more about me and the work I do with modern mamas of young children, you can find me at dawnwarrior.com.

Most importantly, I am so excited to be sharing this knowledge and wisdom with you and helping you remember the truth of who you really are.

Learning The Dawn Warrior Way quite literally changed my life. I know it will change yours, too.

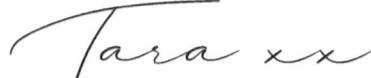

A GIFT FOR YOU

By choosing to journey along the Dawn Warrior path, you are saying "yes" to the call of your soul.

I would love to honour your courage by sharing one of my limited-edition prints with you – *Warrior: One Morning at a Time* will inspire you to realise your worth.

This full-glorious-colour, downloadable A4 print is valued at $27, and it is my gift to you... from my mama heart to yours.

Head here to download your beautiful gift:

dawnwarrior.com/bookgift

INTRODUCTION

Mums are used to running themselves into the ground. Most of us accept stress as the price we have to pay for being a mother. Consider Emma. She runs a successful business from home. When her graphic design business finally took off last year, she was thrilled to be suddenly in demand and she gave it her all. With two young children, a household to run, and the late nights ("Just one more hour, honey!") she is always on the verge of exhaustion, alternating between keyed-up adrenalin and worry that her children and husband are getting the short end of the stick.

She doesn't remember the last time she experienced a deep sleep or had a day when she was relaxed. She hasn't exercised in a month. She grabs quick snacks during the day and often finds herself finishing off an entire block of chocolate at 2am, right before she turns off the computer. One night, head in her hands, Emma decides to go to bed early (before midnight), leaving her client's logo design to be completed in the morning. At 4am, her three-year-old wakes up with a fever and without realising it she screams, "You can't be sick, Oliver! Not today, please!"

He cries and Emma feels like a terrible mother.

I've got it covered

I've always been ambitious, with energy to spare. With a successful career in the competitive events industry, I travelled abroad from Australia and served as an organiser for the Olympic Winter Games. My husband used to joke about my ability to organise everything down to the last micro detail and I would chuckle. Hey, I knew I had it covered and I loved nothing more than taking on a new challenge to prove it.

A few years later – after a miscarriage and three years of fertility treatments – I found myself with two children under the age of two, thinking, "How am I supposed to do it all – mumming, wife-ing, business owning, house managing, meal cooking – and still make it out alive?" The stress reached a breaking point when my daughter, Sienna, was diagnosed with silent reflux.

I had lost control of my days, and like Emma and many other mums, I stopped taking care of myself. My husband had to remind me to take a shower and wash the maternity jeans that I threw on every morning. (I loved those jeans because they were the ones that covered what I called my "mama belly".) Battling my never-ending to-do list, I had no energy or creativity left to focus on developing a business idea I'd had while pregnant with Sienna. In fact, my idea now seemed like a fantasy, a dream I'd had in another world.

The morning is the best part of the day

One late night while standing at my desk (I rarely made time to sit down anymore), I was putting away some files when my eyes fell upon a photo of my grandfather, Reg, whose loss I was still mourning. His face stopped me: the sparkle in his eye and that playful smile... it was as if he knew the secret of life.

INTRODUCTION

I thought of the wonderful lessons I had learned from him. He always insisted on toasting life's celebrations and believed in the importance of trying to make others smile. But the life-changing lesson he taught me was the value and magic of the morning. He was fond of saying that the morning was the best part of the day, and he never let it go by without welcoming it. Without fail, he would start his day with a walk to the local shop to get the newspaper and then spend an hour reading and enjoying his coffee. We all knew never to interrupt him. That was his special time.

I recalled my travelling days, when I used to wake early, take time to get centred and enjoy the peace of the morning. When did I stop doing that?

The next morning, I rose before the first light, padded into the kitchen, made a cup of coffee, and walked out to the deck. I watched the horizon begin to brighten, pulled up the wicker chair and sipped slowly until my cup was empty and the sky was orange. Something that felt like "peace" descended on me.

It had been a long time.

The Dawn Warrior Way

I started getting up early before anyone stirred. I still felt stressed and overwhelmed, and often irritated. I knew that one magic morning wasn't going to fix my life but I kept going, inspired by my grandfather. Gradually, one morning at a time, my life began to change. Before I had the words for it, I had decided to become a Dawn Warrior.

As most mums discover early on, motherhood requires resources beyond the ordinary. That's because becoming a mother is more than a lifestyle change; it marks the beginning of a major life passage. The experience alters her completely and demands a new source of strength and courage – the qualities inherent in warriors. I'm not talking about the so-called warriors of movies, who train for glory or recognition, but the true warriors who live by principles and a code of honour. Like a true warrior, you rise to the challenge of overcoming obstacles and protecting those around you, as well as protecting yourself. You use tools and practices that lift you above the fight or flight reactions of mounting stress, reactions that can quickly lead to exhaustion. Know that the Dawn Warrior path is not for the faint of heart. It requires total commitment to listen to, and connect deeply with, your emerging self. The realisation that this type of dedication and determination is required can be a huge catalyst for positive change. The warrior trains to be prepared to defend what she loves. It is part of her spirit, her mind and her being.

The qualities of a Dawn Warrior

A Dawn Warrior is a woman who is mentally strong, pursues her life passions and honours her motherly spirit. She rises with the dawn and radiates, one morning at a time. She lets in the full light of the day, which lifts her to the higher ground of consciousness. She creates a sanctuary for herself to drink in the nourishment of each new day, a daily oasis that allows her the space and time to create a purposeful, joy-filled and wholehearted life. She is a happy mum.

Sound like wishful thinking? A far-fetched fantasy?

Not at all. In fact, these results are based on a proven life-design system I developed, refined and put into practice over a few years. Hard work, continual research, and consistency in practising this system have made it possible for me to live the life I desired – a life in which I am a meditation teacher, life counsellor for mums, yoga enthusiast, author and business owner. What's more, I have had success in all areas: health, wealth, business and love – without the guilt.

Design your life

The first phase of any life passage may start with a life crisis. A mum finds herself on a precipice with no path going forward – and, in these modern times, no guide. She desperately needs a wise teacher – a warrior – to teach her about the path ahead of her. This is your call to awaken and redesign your life. I encourage you to discover the value of having a life-design system that offers you a step-by-step approach with practical tools to create a happy, healthy and purposeful life. (It's a bit more than just having a cup of coffee in the morning.) Your success is not about becoming a perfect person, wife or parent, entrepreneur or artist. It's about finding your true centre and celebrating it. It's about finding your greatness, the "more" you were created for. The dream, vision or idea that makes your heart flutter with excitement while also giving you a sense of inner peace. A path with heart, meaning and purpose.

Wherever you find yourself in your journey, I get it. There's no judgement here. But one thing I know is that you have a choice: you can actively design every area in your life, including your health, wellbeing, marriage, career and family. The first step, the crucial beginning, is to look at how you are using your time.

Dawn Warrior lifts off the weight from modern mamas by revealing a way to establish and grow a powerful daily routine – this long-term habit serves as an anchor through every season of motherhood.

Discover how to:

* Design a life plan that complements your beliefs, values and goals (rather than what the rest of the world says to do)

* Find what "lights you up" and makes you jump out of bed every day
* Greet the day with your own personalised, adaptable morning ritual that embraces what you're here to do
* Be the best version of yourself by loving yourself and your unique gifts
* Thrive in being an exceptional role model for your children and community

Doesn't that sound amazing? Did you sigh with contentment (or relief) and sink into your chair when you read that list? I'm honoured to share my system with you, because I know that it has the potential to transform your life.

The buried secret

There's a little secret that most of us know deep down inside ourselves but that is forgotten under the burden of stress and exhaustion. As mums, if we neglect our own wellbeing, we will have less and less energy to draw from, reduced compassion and not enough love to give – whether to our family, our work or our community. This life-altering understanding came to me one morning a few months after a crisis had passed and I had started doing my favourite yoga stretches again. In that pre-dawn stillness, it became clear that if I was going to have a successful business and marriage – *and* raise happy children – I needed to be happy first.

About getting your life back… You can't actually go back and get it, can you? And you don't need to. You can create a new life based on a new self. This emerging self will allow you to tap into a fresh – and limitless – well of energy deep within you, deep enough to carry you through the day and beyond. It's time to ask yourself: what do you want to experience in this lifetime? What

INTRODUCTION

legacy do you want to leave? What do you want your kids to remember you for?

This book is my invitation to you. Don't settle. When the world tells you to just be happy with what you have and be grateful for every blessing you've received, take the advice; but understand that there is more.

Let's get started!

PART 1

THE DAWN & THE WARRIOR

One can make a day of any size, and regulate the rising and setting of his own sun and the brightness of its shining.

John Muir

CHAPTER 1

A DEEPER DIVE INTO MY STORY

I was lying on my back, staring at the monitor. The lights were dimmed, and the monitor glowed in the darkness. The room felt cold and my body shivered. The day was 24 April 2014. I was 29 years old and about 11 weeks' pregnant. It was my first scan and I was here alone.

The young sonographer left the room and returned shortly with another sonographer, one who was older and whom I assumed was her supervisor. She lifted the wand from the machine and rubbed it over my tummy as the younger one had done only minutes earlier. I strained to make out the picture, but before I could see the image clearly the screen went black, and she was putting back the instrument and wiping off the cold gel. The room instantly felt colder. She placed her hand gently on my arm.

"I'm so sorry but there is no heartbeat."

"Excuse me, what did you say?"

"There is no heartbeat, dear."

I asked again and she repeated the same words.

"What do you mean, there is no heartbeat?"

She looked at me sadly.

My body tensed and my heart started pumping frantically. I heard her say something about a follow-up procedure but I couldn't process her words. Instead, along with wild beating in my chest, I was acutely aware of my surroundings: the low hum of the machine, the faint noise of voices outside the door. She helped me to sit up and then walked me back to the nook where my jacket and handbag were waiting. I sat down on the chair and started to shake. I wrapped my arms around my shaking body and the heart-wrenching pain filled me. I was drowning.

Where was my husband?

Then I remembered. We both had decided that since he had an important board meeting, there was no need for him to lose a day of work. *Because, of course, everything would be fine and wonderful.*

I cried uncontrollably and when I tried to stand I fell back onto the chair and cried some more. A piercing headache started that would last for weeks, as would my nausea and raw, red eyes.

This wasn't the plan. This wasn't how my story was supposed to go.

The next few weeks dragged by slowly, much of the time spent with tears streaming down my face. This happened whether I was making a cup of tea, holding onto my husband, hugging my dog, staring at the wall or setting the dinner table. *What had happened?* There had been no spotting, no pain. The doctor said it was classified as a "missed miscarriage". After surgery, we continued to hope.

Three months passed but I wasn't getting a period; an exam revealed I had Asherman's syndrome, which is where scar tissue forms in the uterus due to some form of trauma. In my case, it was caused by the dilation and curettage (D&C) surgical procedure I had undergone. I was told I would never be able to fall pregnant again. It was heartbreaking, and I refused to believe it. Not one to give up easily (or at all, as my husband often says), I spent the next three years undergoing countless fertility treatments, acupuncture, detox programs and other surgical procedures – whatever it took to realise our desire for a family.

Early ambitions

From the beginning, I was an achiever. I grew up learning how to read and play music, dance jazz ballet and ballroom, swim every stroke, throw a javelin and much more. From ballroom dancing medals to sports captain, achieving was in my blood. My parents taught me to be an all-rounder. So much so that when it came to my career I was uncertain of which path to take. I enjoyed everything from health, fitness and science to business management. I enrolled in a sports science degree at university and in my first couple of years, I struggled. I loved the content but for some reason wasn't getting the marks I was hoping for, and the idea of working in a lab terrified me. I reconsidered my options and transferred to events and business.

My work in events involved diving into the worlds of tourism and hospitality and it also took me overseas to the Olympic Winter Games. I loved the versatility, the diversity of people and the excitement. I flourished with the opportunities to develop my talents in planning, budgeting, creating and designing. I thought I loved it, but I also felt something was missing. After years of climbing the corporate ladder, I came to realise my place in events management didn't embody my purpose and "light me up". I chose this work because it paid well, and it made me feel as though I was successful. But more than that, it was something that my extended family was happy about. I sacrificed what I wanted for the sake of people around me. I didn't want to hurt them, and I didn't want them to be uncomfortable around me, so instead I picked a career not based on what I truly felt inside.

The magic of mornings

By the time the third year of IVF treatment rolled around, I was deeply depressed and overweight – and I was definitely tired of going to the baby showers of my friends while trying to hide my despair. One afternoon, after coming home from one more baby shower, tears rolling down my face, I sat down and looked at myself in the mirror. I asked, "Why am I hiding from the world? Why can I not accept myself the way I am? Why am I bringing an energy of 'not accepting' to the world? Instead, what if I was the 'whole me'? And what would my ideal life look like – with or without kids?"

I didn't know the answer.

Shortly after that came the life-changing night when I stumbled across the photo of my grandfather Reg, which served as a constant reminder to me of the magic of mornings. How long had it been since I had paid any attention to my morning routine? The very next day, I started back.

Gradually, one morning at a time, clarity began to emerge.

I went through every area of my life in great detail to work out my beliefs, values and vision – and after evaluating my knowledge and skills, I realised I wanted to start my own business. I had a lot of doubts but I went ahead and developed an event planning toolkit, left my full-time job and became a freelance event planner. I also decided to have one more go at having a baby, through surrogacy, and if that failed my husband and I would accept it. But first, we needed some time to prepare ourselves for this step, financially and mentally. So we sold our house in Brisbane and moved to the Sunshine Coast.

In three short months – we couldn't believe it – I fell pregnant naturally. No treatments, no acupuncture, no procedures. It was a wondrous feeling. From the exhilarating moment when I shared the news with my husband, to the nerve-wracking 12 weeks that followed, to finally reaching full term and birthing a beautiful boy into this world, fears of miscarriage haunted me. I didn't "breathe easy" throughout the whole pregnancy. Once I held my son in my hands I was able to breathe again. And when we named him, it seemed only fitting to use my grandfather's name as his middle name.

As the weeks passed with my newborn son, the realities of motherhood set in. Living away from friends and family, and with my husband travelling four hours to work each day, I raised my son solo in the first year, with limited support. I did my best to navigate the all-encompassing motherhood journey, barely keeping my head above water. If you're a mother, I'm sure you know the feeling: the thrill of being a mother can quickly turn to overwhelm. My life at this time was characterised by bouts of depression, perfectionism, worry, isolation and playing "Miss Fix-It" to everyone else but me. What I came to realise was that, like almost all mothers, I had stopped dedicating time to focus on myself. And even when I managed to sneak a few moments for myself (which was extremely rare) I was racked by guilt and feelings that I was being "selfish" – that I was neglecting my motherly duties. This feeling of lack of control and connection to myself led to me spiralling back into depression, which I thought I had put behind me.

One afternoon, while pacing up and down the hallway in the hopes of getting my son to sleep, I fell to the ground, sobbing. I thought, "Is this what my life looks like now?" I knew I had been feeling reluctant to speak to my husband or anyone else about this because I didn't want to seem ungrateful for being a mother.

Later that night, I was going through my journal and I came across some wisdom I had written down: "Pain and suffering are part of the human condition. But they don't define our life. What defines our life is what we do when we encounter pain and suffering. Challenges are learning opportunities – it's where we grow". In that moment, I thought, "I have a choice – to carry on with my life as it is or to begin to make a change". I could choose to put my life on hold and just keep my head above water for the next 10 years (until the kids are older). Or, I could acknowledge that I had changed since becoming a mother, and that I could choose to take a step back, look at my life and become crystal clear on who I am and what makes me happy.

"Reality" then crept in, and I asked myself, "How would I manage to do this? Would I earn enough money to live on if I followed my dreams instead of being 'practical'? What about the children's futures?" Then something clicked into place. I pushed all of those concerns aside and made the decision to do things differently, no matter what. I may not have known what changes I would make, but I did know that I didn't want to carry on exactly as I had been.

By this time in our lives, my husband and I had walked through two miscarriages, countless disappointments and emotional chaos, and we had learned so much about ourselves as a couple and as individuals. However, this all-encompassing identity shift, this major life passage I was experiencing... I had never imagined that my life would so abruptly change within just a few months of becoming a mother. After reflecting on the pain and suffering I had been experiencing, and the choice I had made to live life differently, it dawned on me. I realised that my morning routine had gone out the window during this first year of motherhood. I had become lost in the mayhem of being a mum.

I discovered that you don't need to know what your longer-term goals are before beginning to live a life that is true to you. As your life unfolds, day by day, you begin to see the road open up in front of you. By choosing to travel along the road that was right for me (a road that became clearer and clearer because of my morning routine), I started to live a fulfilling and blessed life. I was also able to fall pregnant naturally (again) with our second child, our beautiful daughter, Sienna. Coincidence? Maybe. But all I knew is that I had been told I would NEVER get pregnant and here I was, pregnant for a SECOND time. I had a truly wonderful natural birth, but the months that followed tested my strength because, in the first few weeks, my daughter developed severe silent reflux. It was especially challenging because doctors were reluctant to prescribe medicine for such a young infant. But after several doctor appointments (with her screaming in pain in the car for the entire journey), we put her on a treatment plan. My husband and I took turns sleeping upright with her for weeks until the treatment started to work.

Did my spirit break during this time? Not completely. Why? My mornings. While the experience of infertility had taught me resilience, it was my morning system that kept me from breaking. Despite the situation, I kept my morning system in place. I had been using my mornings to heal my mind, body and soul for years – on and off – but this time I committed myself and I did not look back – although I did adjust it to accommodate the extra responsibilities of having a newborn.

Core identity

One day in the shower I was pondering on my passions and life purpose, and it clicked for me. I realised exactly what I wanted to do with my life! It felt like an energy rush over my body and it brought me instantly to happy tears. I hopped out of the shower, grabbed my towel, padded – still wet – down the hallway to my desk, grabbed pen and paper and started to write everything down. I couldn't stop. A wave of inspiration caught me and I had to follow it because if I didn't I knew it would fly straight past me.

I wrote: "Working with mothers to help them realise that to create the most positive impact in their lives is first to create the blueprint for how to be the best version of themselves and then to live that every day". I had a visual of this – a massive group of women covered in armour walking up towards a bright light, which looked like the sun rising. The words "50,000 Dawn Warriors" came to me.

Discovering my purpose didn't happen overnight, but once I started to take those initial steps towards what lights me up, I really started to understand what lay ahead for me. I found that your heart is your best tool for accessing your true purpose and passion – when guided by your heart, you are naturally more joyful and motivated to explore. And I also realised that my purpose has taken shape into many things, not just the ONE thing. It's morphed into helping mothers, helping children and eventually helping their families. So we need to let go of the notion of there being only "one"' purpose for each of us.

It was through goal setting and habit synergy, along with implementing tools for healing and spiritual growth, when things really started to take off. Through the power of my mornings, I was able to sustain my sanity and raise two kids under the age of two… and achieve so much more. My mornings became my saving grace. They became the foundation for being the best mum and wife I could be. But it went further than that. With the stability and control of my morning routine, I overcame my depression and poor eating habits and lost 8kg. I quickly became healthier, happier and more vibrant, with a clear direction in my life. I had time again to go after my passions and complete my studies.

Birthing the Dawn Warrior

I was just glowing as a new mother, and other mums were noticing. They were curious about how I managed to thrive while raising my son and staying up all night with my daughter. So, I told these fellow mums my story and showed them how to introduce my morning system into their lives. Although they were intrigued, they were also understandably a little sceptical, and unsure if they could fit a morning routine into their hectic lives. However, they gave it a try. Soon they, too, started seeing similar results to mine. Stress levels plummeted; creativity flourished; families became happier. I then thought that if this could help a couple of mums, perhaps it could help more? So I took everything I had learned, researched and experienced, and developed The Dawn Warrior Way.

I had created a way that any busy mum can build her own daily morning ritual, radiate intention, develop awareness and take empowered action. More than that, I had designed it in a way that makes it incredibly easy to introduce into even the most hectic "mum schedule". (Because I KNOW how crazy things can be.) I now had *evidence* that it worked for other women.

So today, when I hear the following question from an exhausted and discouraged mum, I have only one response.

Is it really possible for me to increase my energy, navigate motherhood with calmness and clarity, and get in touch with my purpose?

You bet it is. Read on to discover how you really can do all of this, and more.

CHAPTER 2

THE FOUR ELEMENTS

"You need to be happy first." For many mums I know and work with, this statement, especially when spoken out loud, can generate intense guilt and feelings of disloyalty. For some, it's just plain-out heresy, evoking that dreaded word: *selfish*. Why? Because it violates a deep-seated belief that your family's needs should come first.

So what you're left with is: not only does the idea of pursuing your own interests and goals seem impossible, it also feels wrong. This is why many mums say to me things like, "I know I have to wait until Chloe's in school and then I can start my business". Substitute whatever it is for you: go back to work, get that certification/degree, pursue your art.

The result of this mindset is that mums accept what seems inevitable and try to fit in their needs as best they can.

The Dawn Warrior mindset

I invite you to consider a different view, that of the Dawn Warrior mindset – it can transform your experience and your ability to create a one-of-a-kind life that works for *you*. First, please understand that this mindset is not a set of beliefs or rules, a rigid way of doing things – it's also not about being perfect (phew!).

The characteristics of a true warrior mindset are clarity, flexibility and bravery. It requires having an awareness of how to thrive, being able to learn and respond flexibly in the face of seemingly overwhelming obstacles, and having the courage to choose what matters most to you. It means allowing yourself to draw on masculine warrior strength.

A warrior understands the power of mind, the strength of body, and the calmness of "now", and trusts in spirit. These qualities are in all of us. Together, they form a powerful energy that you can draw upon every day and in every circumstance. This energy requires cultivation and nurturing. That's why warriors train: to align with mission, self and spirit.

Becoming a Dawn Warrior is not just about reducing stress, saving time or becoming more efficient, though these are welcome and wonderful results. It's bigger than that. It's about discovering and unleashing what's in your core, your heart – not unlike the daily bursting forth of the dawn.

A Dawn Warrior claims her power, knows her goal and takes the steps to rapidly turn her vision into reality. When I began to practise this mindset consistently, I overcame infertility, depression and an eating disorder, and went on to design the life I wanted. An empowered mindset absolutely underpins success. Without it, you won't take the actions that will create real change.

Why be a warrior?

Mums I've spoken with have realised that the transition to motherhood has awoken them to new possibilities in life, and enabled them to find new strengths within themselves. This transition also acts as a catalyst for a mother's desire to live more authentically. It creates an opportunity to re-tell her life story, align it with her goals and values and create greater coherence in her life.

We all seek to discover our authenticity – living a life that is not true to oneself causes distress and lies at the heart of many problems. Most of us make decisions or choose our life's direction based on what we've been told will create a nice income or a comfortable life. We follow what our friends, family and society expect us to do. We make choices according to what matters to us at the time. This is the way most people live, and there's nothing wrong with it. However, making choices with intention, forethought and authenticity is vital to all aspects of your life: your wellbeing, the success of your relationships, how your career unfolds and how you feel when you look back on your life.

The more we are able to be ourselves, the happier we will be. And the happier we are, the more we contribute to the betterment of those around us. However, if our needs go unfulfilled, the more distressed, damaged and dysfunctional we become and the more we contribute to the destructive forces of the world.

Our world needs more Dawn Warriors – awakened women and empowered mothers. A Dawn Warrior is a woman, a mum, who wants more, sees more and is ready to challenge herself to turn her dream into reality. In fact, it's time to discover your quest. A quest is bigger than a goal. It is a life dream that involves your whole being and engages your spirit. When unleashed, it has unbelievable power because a quest comes from your core identity.

Your core identity

I believe everyone has two versions of themselves. The first is the identity you walk around with that's made up of roles – you're the lawyer, the mother, the designer, the business owner. This is, however, only the shell. It's the role you're playing in the world, and most probably it's the role you've been playing for someone else. It's the role you chose to play so that you fit into conventional society. But this is not you. There is a second version of you. The person you secretly desire to be. This is your core identity. This realisation puts you on the path to becoming a Dawn Warrior.

Our core identity is always trying to inform the outer world of the next evolution. Our deepest core desires are never limited to goals about making money or developing a great network. Those things are surface outcomes and your brain is lying to you when it tells you that you are those outcomes. The truth is this: the whole point of being human is to create experiences. If you think about what you want in life, you will probably find that it's not about money or wealth; it's about experiences. Whether it's the experience of travel, living in a gorgeous home, watching your children thrive or making love to that special someone.

My life dream is to ignite collective potential so that we feel more connected to ourselves, each other and nature. I'm on a mission to inspire feminine bravery and let our beautiful lives unfold.

The four elements revealed

To develop a Dawn Warrior mindset, you need four elements. In parts 2 and 3, we'll dive deeper into each of these elements:

THE FOUR ELEMENTS

1. Discover your purpose
2. Live consciously in all areas of your life
3. Create your life plan and commit to it
4. Harness the dawn

Here's a sneak peek into each element:

1. Discover your purpose

This is about getting clear on your true needs and desires. There is a lot of information out there telling you exactly what you need to do. However, what works for one person won't necessarily work for all. By setting clear intentions you put on blinders that allow you to ignore what everyone else is doing and focus on your own journey. No one knows what you need more than you do.

2. Live consciously in all areas of your life

It is important to cultivate awareness. The more aware we are in any situation, the more possibilities we tend to perceive, the more options we have and the more powerful we are. Living consciously means seeking to be aware of everything that affects our actions, purposes, values and goals – and behaving with intention. If you ever do something without actively thinking about it, you are not living consciously.

3. Create your life plan & commit to it

Whatever goals you have, large or small, you'll need to believe in yourself and create a clear path to achieve those goals. Whether you want to earn more to take the kids on a holiday or start your dream business from home, you need to commit to taking consistent, purposeful action.

The Four Elements

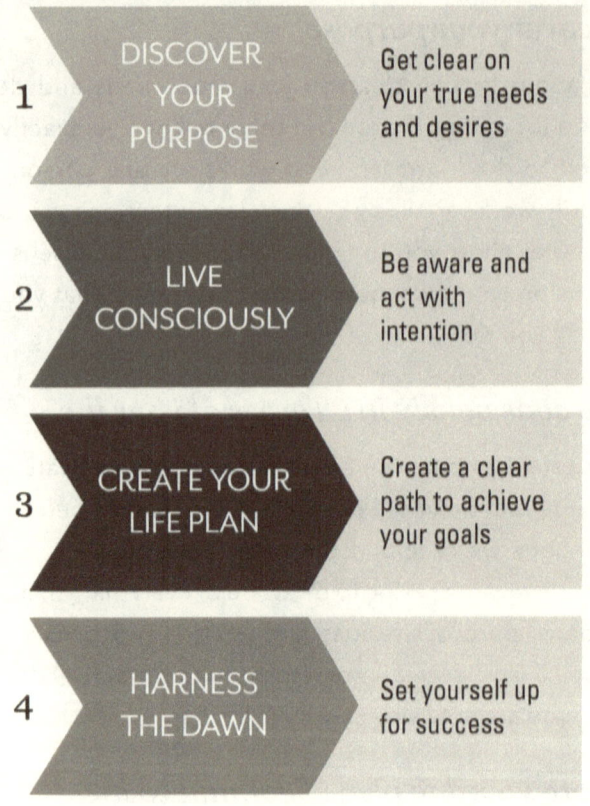

4. Harness the dawn

This element is a special way of setting yourself up for success. There's a reason why successful women like Oprah and Ariana Huffington use the first hour of their day to set themselves up for success: it works. Designing your mornings gives you the ability to be the best version of yourself and the best role model for your kids.

A victim no more

When you decide to be a Dawn Warrior, you no longer view yourself as a victim of circumstances you can't control. You know you have the choice to shape your life. Once you learn how to show up for yourself and do the inner work, you realise and accept that it takes bravery, strength and self-compassion to become the most empowered version of yourself.

CHAPTER 3

AWAKEN YOUR INNER VOICE

On the morning that my grandfather Reg left this earth, I climbed a mountain – in my sixth month of pregnancy with my son, Austin – to watch the sun rise. The night before I had packed my bag with water, camera, phone and a picture of Reg. At the base of the mountain, I received a call. I knew what the call was going to be and the words that would be spoken: "Reg has passed". He had been unwell, but we thought he would pull through... With tears rolling down my face, I climbed to the top and watched the first light spill over the clouds and spread over the earth. A truly majestic moment.

We all have thoughts that come to us throughout the day but your inner voice is not just an everyday thought; it carries a message that awakens and stirs something inside you. This life-changing experience has happened a few times in my life and I've learned to listen. Deeper than a gut instinct, these nudges come from the deepest, most authentic part of ourselves.

"You can't run a business"

Sometimes we ignore or dismiss these intuitive messages offhandedly as being impractical or unimportant. When I first got the idea of starting a business, my resistance and doubt immediately chimed in, "You can't do that. You can't run a business". But the idea didn't go away; it kept coming back, no matter how many times I dismissed it. So one morning, I decided to test it out on my husband.

"I'm going to start my own business," I said, matter-of-factly.

At that moment I remember looking at him, measuring his reaction. I expected to see his face say, "Really?" with a look of doubt or scepticism. Instead, he smiled and gave me a nod, which surprised me. Later, I realised that people respond more to HOW we say things than to WHAT we actually say.

The truth was I didn't know if I was capable of owning a business. And if I was capable, I had no idea when or how it could happen.

Waking up

Something interesting happens when you start tapping into your inner voice. You notice messages you would otherwise miss: desires and longings that lay beneath the surface, waiting to wake us up. Some of these messages come in the form of coincidences and jealousy. Coincidences encourage us to recognise the ideas within us that we might not be registering on a conscious level. They help us identify deeper desires. Have you ever had a conversation with someone and later found the same conversation popping up somewhere else? When you start uncovering the things that light you up, don't be surprised when they start showing up all over the place!

Jealousy is not a dirty word in my world. Like coincidences, jealousy is often a gift, acting as an internal compass to point us in the direction of our desires. The key is not to allow jealous feelings to get out of control, but to be aware of them and where they're showing up. You will likely encounter jealousy in the face of other people's possessions, accomplishments, career advancement, marital status, spouses, holidays, children, friends, what they've eaten for lunch and their adorable pup posted all over Instagram.

Take heart; this is normal. It's also normal to try to shut down these negative thoughts because we think jealousy is bad, when in fact we need to be digging up the roots of its existence and looking closer. Getting upset about what we don't have and why we don't have it is often needed to figure out how our lives have to shift in order to pursue a path that opens richer possibilities. It's an opportunity to get clear on what you desire and why you're here.

Tuning in to your true voice

When I say "true voice", I don't mean our inner critic or the constant worrying that keeps us awake at night. We must learn to block out all that mental noise and hear our own inner voice of wisdom. At first it might only be a faint whisper. We soon begin to realise that behind those worrying thoughts and critical remarks is another voice that belongs to us. By listening carefully we can begin to trust that voice to be our reliable compass, encouraging us to follow our intended purpose. We were given one life and it will take this lifetime to live out our purpose. Perhaps you've felt a divine nudge before, or maybe you haven't. Regardless, these nudges are inside us all; we just need to become quiet enough to hear them.

When you're talking or busy with life, listening to your soul won't happen. The key to receiving these messages is to create space for them through silence, which is difficult these days, especially for mums. Most of us are busy and only getting busier. As a society, we are driven to keep accomplishing, to be productive all the time. To take time for silence or contemplation is not valued or encouraged.

But there's a time and a place for everything, and if you want to hear your inner voice, you need stillness and awareness.

I was not a quiet child, a quiet teen or a quiet young adult. For most of my life, I never liked being alone and I enjoyed attention. It's surprising that I actually heard these nudges at all. It seems to me that valuing stillness is a lesson that most of us learn sooner or later. I wish I had learned sooner to be more aware of my own inner voice of wisdom. And I am still learning, day by day, to listen to it more. Steve Jobs said in an address to graduating students at Stanford University: "Your time is limited, so don't waste it living someone else's life ... Don't let the noise of others' opinions drown out your own inner voice. And most important, have the courage to follow your heart and intuition. They somehow already know what you truly want to become. Everything else is secondary". Steve Jobs' words are probably the best advice anyone can ever hear for how to live their life. He may not have known it, but his words echo the best thinking of today.

Your purpose matters

We are all born with unique and wonderful gifts. Your inner voice, that little voice, is YOU. It knows why you are here and what you are called to do. It knows the life you were designed to live and what gifts you have to make this world a better place. There's a whole plan we are all a part of and you have a very specific role to play – no one but you can fill that role. This tiny voice is pushing you to uncover who that beautiful magical person is inside.

Most of us live each day assuming we'll grow old and enjoy a lifetime on this planet. We don't pursue our passion because, hey, there's always another day. Eventually, we stop dreaming that we are made for more. Though I don't know you personally, I can tell you with 100% certainty that you were made to be great. No one has your story, your background or your unique gifts. You're the only you and the world needs you now.

The calling to follow your heart comes from within and no one can hear it but you. At first, it may be a small stirring, a faint voice, a strange idea. This calling usually doesn't come from a place of logic and reason; it emerges from a place of authentic truth and soul intuition. Are you ready to follow it?

CHAPTER 4

THE LAW OF ATTRACTION

After first starting an early morning ritual, I realised that I was onto something when I began to wake up with energy, intention and purpose every single day. Despite the life obstacles that came my way, I noticed I was always fairly optimistic and felt surprisingly replenished. My daily practices of exercise and meditation enabled me to achieve incredible results in my life, including overcoming the hardships and disappointments of miscarriage and failed infertility treatments, and the resulting depression.

I must confess, I haven't always had the best relationships with mornings. In my childhood and teenage years, and even in university, I was the person who hit the snooze bar two or three times, flew out of bed, grabbed an apple from the fridge and ran out the door at the last minute. It wasn't the best way to start my mornings. However, when I later became a morning person, I discovered the positive effects that came from rising earlier.

After realising the power of the morning, I spent the next few years reading about morning routines, including the tips and tricks for how to get up and how to use the time effectively. This came from reading Robin Sharma's *The 5AM Club* and Hal Elrod's *The Miracle Morning*, and looking obsessively into famous people's routines (like those of Ariana Huffington and Oprah Winfrey, to name a few). It wasn't until I came across a study by the Medical Research Council – another one of those coincidences! – which revealed a correlation between rising early and greater wellbeing along with a lower risk of depression, that I thought about turning my experience into something for others to benefit from. Then I became curious and wondered if there was additional research and, yes, there was.

Biologist Christopher Randler discovered, and published in the *Harvard Business Review*, that early risers are more proactive and more likely to anticipate problems and minimise them efficiently. He writes: "People whose performance peaks in the morning are better positioned for career success, because they're more proactive than people who are at their best in the evening".

Then there's the University of Barcelona study that compared early risers with night owls. According to this 2014 comparative study, early risers tend to be more resistant to fatigue and more resilient when faced with problems than night owls. This, in turn, makes them less prone to depression, anxiety and substance abuse.

After discovering this research, I started to break down my method and developed the Dawn Warrior concept. To really provide value, I also studied the work of pioneering life philosophers, leaders in social psychology and behavioural change, and authors such as Marcus Aurelius, Thích Nhất Hạnh, Florence Scovel Shinn, Dalai Lama, Deepak Chopra, Joe Dispenza, Stephen Covey, Joe Vitali, Michael Beckwith, Brené Brown and Rhonda Byrne.

And I discovered the Law of Attraction.

"Like" attracts "like"

The Secret, by Rhonda Byrne, is a popular movie and book that identifies a way of thinking that embodies what's commonly called the Law of Attraction. Watching this inspiring film many years ago (and undertaking more research since then) made me realise that my success had come directly from how I was using my mind. What I discovered was: what you think about, you bring about. What you think about becomes your belief. What you believe becomes your perception of life. And your perception determines your experience.

Where you place your focus can have an immense impact on what happens to you. Whether or not we realise it, we are responsible for bringing both positive and negative influences into our lives *through the thoughts we hold on to and consistently repeat*. If you think of where you want to be then you'll naturally start to take actions to get there. You'll see that you are not a victim and that you have the freedom to take control of your future and shape it the way you want.

To start attracting what you want, the first step is to get clear on your current focus. Ask yourself:

* Where am I putting my energy?
* What are my predominant thoughts throughout the day?
* What kinds of conversations am I having?
* Do I spend time complaining, gossiping or criticising others?

My brother's miracle

Ten years ago, my older brother Aaron was hit by a car. He broke his neck and was in a coma for two weeks in intensive care. When he came out of the coma and started breathing by himself, he was moved to a spinal ward. The doctors told our family that he was never going to walk again, that he would be "like Christopher Reeve". The news shocked us all. To help his body gain some movement and build muscle, he went through an intense rehabilitation program. We spent many months talking with him, feeding him and just being there with him. Every time I saw him, he would always say, "Tara, I have a strong self-healing power and I am going to walk out of this hospital".

Each night as he fell asleep, he told his brain to move his big toe. He chose his toe because it was the furthest point from his brain. If he could get a message to travel from his brain to his toe, then he could move every other part of his body, too. After months of this, the moment came: his big toe moved. He couldn't believe it. He beamed with pure joy and delight, and this was only the beginning. He soon moved his hands, his arms and his legs and gained enough strength to sit up. A year later, my brother walked out of that hospital. He had achieved the impossible.

With the unwavering repetition of positive thought and action, he had gained mental strength. His intention to recover his ability to walk became unshakable. What I realised later was that *in his mind* he was already there; he just had to wait for his body to gain the muscle strength to do it.

Is it just wishful thinking?

Many people view recovery "miracles" like my brother's as simply unexplainable. Surely, they argue, it's not possible for something as flimsy as "positive thought" to regenerate a spinal cord (or any other physical function). There must have been an underlying condition that doctors weren't aware of that allowed him to walk again.

GOLDEN HOUR AFFIRMATION

ALL THAT I AM INSPIRES
ALL THAT I WILL BE

#DAWNWARRIOR

I think it's important to examine such claims and so I spent some time looking into the available research.

What I discovered was the notion of mind–body medicine, which focuses on the role of the mind in illness and health. It acknowledges that a direct relationship exists and that the body's innate healing potential is initiated by the mind. As a therapy, it has emerged as an integral part of health care. It has also given rise to the legitimisation of research, and the incorporation of mind–body programs in the work of major medical institutions. Thus, scientists have developed a new discipline called psychoneuroimmunology, which links psychological, autonomic, immune and nervous system performance. Current mind–body medicine extends beyond psychoneuroimmunology to include the fields of psychology and physics in a new "science of consciousness", which recognises energy as the underlying pattern of the universe.

As I continued to develop my system, my morning ritual strengthened and I witnessed the steady shifting of my identity. By placing intention on a certain area, I witnessed how the universe shaped itself around that intention, often in surprising, unexpected ways. Specifically, I began to focus my energy on creating more space in my life through journaling and reflection on my goals (more about this process in part 3).

The universe fulfils your intention

Thoughts become things. Whatever you're longing for, whatever your dreams and goals, the Law of Attraction can bring it into your life. This law is not just for some "special" people – it is meant for you. When you start to connect deeply with your life vision on an ongoing basis, you will attract positive experiences, and over time your ideal future will create itself through you.

When you're a charismatic individual you'll naturally draw praise, warmth and positive attention from those around you. Because you are one with the life-energy you start to experience miracles large and small. You begin to realise and appreciate what you are capable of. For instance, I once entered a competition where the prize was a trip to Sydney. I yearned to visit my good friend Luisa who lives in Sydney. A month later, I received notification that I was the winner and was given a travel voucher for $250, which covered my round-trip flight to Sydney almost to the dollar. My thoughts had become reality.

Taking the Law of Attraction one step further, one of the most powerful things I have realised, over time, is that your experience is actually shaped by your identity. The world doesn't give you what you wish for or want; it gives you WHO you think you are. That's why so many people fail at goal setting or vision boards or creative visualisation – if what you want does not match who you are, the universe will resist you.

Identity-shifting

When we create a massive change in how we see ourselves in relation to the world, we are shifting our identity. Even though I am a firm believer in the Law of Attraction, I also believe that identity-shifting is the thing that can really turbocharge our lives.

I experienced an identity shift when I became a mother. Motherhood made me realise that I had to shed some old behaviours, relationships and environments that I'd grown accustomed to and replace them with new ones. I had to confront many unknowns in order to evolve into a better version of myself. I moved from a place of listening to others who were telling me what I "should" or "shouldn't" be doing during pregnancy and in regards to raising children, and instead I let my heart lead the way – I always felt supported when I followed my intuition. Every time I stood firmly rooted in my new choices and beliefs, miracles emerged and visions of which I once dreamed became my reality.

It was while reading Napoleon Hill's book *Think and Grow Rich* that I began to realise how I had blindly adopted the "people-pleaser" attitude and had a fear of criticism. I was constantly thinking, "Why doesn't this person like me? I didn't do anything to them; all I am trying to do is help others". I'd spend hours worrying about what I should do differently next time so that they would like me. But you cannot please everyone. This awakening immediately caused the notion of "everyone should like me" to lose all of its power. I realised that what other people think of me is none of my business. Allowing myself to let go of that worry was extremely liberating and freed up so much energy – and little miracles, like connecting with business mentors, started to appear in my life. But this awakening also came with a small internal shake-up because it caused my old world to disappear and a new expanded world to unfold. The shake-up eventually settled, but this motherhood "growth" was an invitation for my soul to be felt, my spirit to be heard and my new identity to shape my world.

I now have a quiet sense of wellbeing and equanimity that comes from within. It's a deep trust in the greater forces of the world of which we are a part. I have a respectful awareness that we don't act alone – that our every thought and deed is part of an interconnected web of humanity and life overall. It's a knowing that everything we experience teaches us something valuable and helps us grow. By continually striving to be a positive influence in the world, we make it a better place not only for ourselves but for everyone around us.

CHAPTER 5

WHAT LIGHTS YOU UP?

As mums, many of us base our decisions on the needs of our family, because those needs are immediate and urgent. However, our own personal desires often go by the wayside. We think, "Later. I'll have time later". Perhaps, like me, you had a desire for a family and now that you're travelling that road, it seems only reasonable (and others are happy to confirm this "common sense" view) that you have to go the distance before you can initiate another life journey such as getting a degree or starting a business.

And yet, it feels limiting and you know you're capable of more.

So – what if, instead of making life decisions based on so-called common sense, we made decisions based on what lights us up? The goal or longing you've tucked away in the back of your mind… the thought or vision that leaps forward occasionally that you are quick to suppress because, well, you think you have to wait.

Maslow's Hierarchy of Needs

There is a lot of information out there telling you exactly what you need to do to lead a fulfilling and successful life. But discovering your purpose is about discovering what lights YOU up, not other people. Perhaps you've heard of Maslow's popular hierarchical theory of human needs? It reveals the universal stages of motivation that all humans go through, starting at the most basic needs and rising to the needs we may have for personal growth (see the diagram on the opposite page).

The theory is that once a person's survival and safety needs are met, they are motivated to seek love and belonging with other people.

Many people think that the highest need in the hierarchy is self-actualisation. However, that's not actually true. Maslow had another piece that was on top of self-actualisation, and that was self-transcendence. He just didn't publish this information widely before he passed away. Self-actualisation is indeed a worthy goal of development, but self-transcendence is truly the "next level" of development; it is other-focused instead of self-focused, and concerns higher goals than those that are self-serving.

A little more detail about each:

* Survival: having air, water, food, shelter, sleep and clothing
* Safety: having personal security, income and health
* Love and belonging: experiencing friendship, intimacy and human connection
* Esteem: earning respect and recognition in society
* Self-actualisation: achieving one's full potential

Maslow's Hierarchy of Needs

* Self-transcendence: seeing life from a higher perspective – experiencing joy, peace and a well-developed sense of awareness

Society has led us to believe that a successful life is based on status, recognition from others, and the reward of money. That's why, in today's world, most people never reach the level of "self-actualisation" or "self-transcendence". Instead, people focus on the second level; that of "esteem". The aim of the Dawn Warrior is self-fulfilment – the only way to achieve that is to *live* out your purpose by becoming the highest version of yourself and continuing to expand to become a person with a strong and free identity. You will know when you discover your purpose because it will make you want to jump out of bed every day.

The time is now

The thoughts and feelings that come from our inner voice and that cause us to say to ourselves, "Someday maybe I can do that" are actually *the things we need to pursue now*. Because there is no someday. You cannot wait for the perfect time to act. The perfect time does not exist and there's no guarantee it ever will.

You are here for a purpose: your existence is not random. No one possesses your unique combination of background, gifts and talents.

Your world needs you to pursue now the inkling that is tugging on your heart.

Let's take it a bit further. Say you decide to explore your purpose more fully, to think deeply about what a meaningful, wholehearted life looks like for you. You clarify your desires and discover what lights you up. Tuning into your dream is exciting and, yes, can also be overwhelming to even *think* about pursuing. When are you going to find the time and the energy? It just doesn't seem practical. And here we are again, back at the nub of the problem: our disinclination to expand and grow. We encounter a resistance based on what most of us have been thoroughly taught: pick a respectable path that will provide you with enough income to live a comfortable life.

But that's not the life of a Dawn Warrior.

Many people try to create a new path by changing their circumstances. After my first miscarriage and the diagnosis of Asherman's syndrome months later, I fell into a deeply depressed state. My husband and I decided to move to the Sunshine Coast, believing the move would bring me out of my depression. What I didn't understand then was that it wasn't enough to change externals. What I needed was a plan for my life. To develop a plan, I had to get very clear about what I wanted. That required focus and energy that I did not have at the time; I had to develop it and discover what was blocking my way, what the actual obstacles were. These obstacles were quite surprising yet also very obvious.

All systems break down

A universal force that governs everyone's life, in addition to the Law of Attraction, is the Law of Entropy, discovered by Sir Isaac Newton. The principle of entropy states that all systems disorganise, disintegrate and move towards chaos. This is why no matter how often or thoroughly you clean your bathroom, it becomes dirty and disorganised again. We see examples of entropy everywhere around us. Buildings left alone become ruins, and erosion eventually reduces mountains to hills. Even our sun will eventually burn out. Every second of every day, entropy is a force that affects everything that exists, including everything in your life, your body, your mind, your relationships and your house. Entropy is constantly working to disorganise every one of these systems.

GOLDEN HOUR
AFFIRMATION

I AM A WORK IN PROGRESS AND I WILL CONTINUE TO UNRAVEL AS I LEARN MY WAY

#DAWNWARRIOR

Entropy wins every time because it is constant. Newton proved that the only thing that counteracts entropy in any closed system is constant positive energy coming in from the outside. For instance, our physical body keeps functioning because we eat, and food creates new energy. Same with brushing our teeth or sustaining a good love relationship – it requires constant energy. You want to be a good parent? You need to show up every day. It doesn't matter what area of life we're talking about, the only way to keep things moving in the right direction is by putting constant energy into the system. The key is that you've got to be absolutely consistent; it must be a lifestyle, not just something you do occasionally. This is where the true challenge lies. You will never build your ideal life in fits and starts, which is the reason people why fail over and over in their efforts to lose weight or get fit. You're never going to excel in any area by winging it. What you need is a steady continuous flow of accomplishments. A rhythm of good things coming into your life every single day, every week, every year.

Begin with your purpose

There are a few good methods that can help guide you to discover your purpose. I invite you to do two mini exercises right now that will get you thinking about what really lights you up.

The first is to look back at the significant events of your life. Close your eyes and remember all of those exhilarating and painful experiences, and realise that those highs and lows shaped your values. Make a list of those values. For instance, I was teased at school, which caused me to be more compassionate to others. When I gave birth to my children, I started valuing connectedness and love in a bigger way. Now, take your list and combine values of similar types into groups. The next step is to name each of these groups and identify the top three that resonate with you. Then, ask yourself:

"Given that I have these values, what can I offer the world?" Try to come up with at least three practical ideas. And here's a clue: your top values generally connect to the healing you want to give to the world because of the pain you experienced. Try to stay in alignment with these values, because they are unique to you. Don't take on other people's values or become distracted by what others have done. Stay true to who you are – no one can imitate your story.

The second method for discovering your purpose is to put two minutes on the clock and immediately start writing down anything that you are passionate about – whatever comes to mind; it doesn't matter. Use the following questions to help prompt you:

- What in your life makes you happy? What are you passionate about? What lights you up from your core?
- How can you contribute to your family, your friends, your colleagues, your city or even the world? You might be drawn to helping people achieve success or overcome adversity. Or to working with children or in the creative or dramatic arts.
- What problem are you interested in solving that will help people's lives? Perhaps you want to contribute to the health of our environment or you have resources, such as knowledge, skills or money, you want to give.

Once the two minutes is up, take a look at your list. You may not as yet have found what you want to do, but it's likely that there is *something* (buried or obvious) that lights you up and has the potential to make you jump out of bed every single day. And every woman's purpose is different. For some women, their purpose may be "knowing that their presence makes someone happy" – and making someone happy can be as simple as offering your time or words of encouragement, or cooking for someone. Or it could be "running community fitness programs" or "designing websites for ethically made brands". It could also come in multiple forms — there may not be just ONE thing that you are meant to do, and it may depend on the life stage that you're in. Perhaps a particular woman is meant to write a cookbook for children (when her own children are young), *and* she is meant to be a parent of a child with disability *and* she is meant to teach adult education classes or build an orphanage in a later life stage. For me, my work centres on helping mothers, but it also includes helping their families. So we need to let go of the notion that there is only one purpose.

Creating a plan

Where do you start? A lifestyle is sustained by daily habits that become embedded patterns. Habits are formed by association — the people we spend time with, the material we read, the programs we watch and the information we listen to. What we surround ourselves with and allow to touch our lives ultimately determines the path we follow and the habits we form. Bad habits can be replaced with good habits, by changing things in our lives. It may mean a change in the people we hang around with, or maybe switching off the TV and picking up a good book to stimulate positive thoughts. Or it could be getting up early and putting on our shoes and going for a walk, or even joining the gym. Anything is possible! I have found that the more I do what is good for me, the less room it leaves for what is not good. Bad habits can be squeezed out and suffocated by focusing on and committing to new good habits.

It's all about cause and effect. If you want to improve any area of your life, no matter what it is — fitness, family, finances — you've got to do something to create that improvement. You've got to become the cause of the effect that you want to create. You've got to change the daily behaviours that will allow you to express your deepest personal desires on an ongoing basis.

But habits aren't enough.

Habits must serve our greater goals in order to "take" – to have power. By setting my intentions in all areas of my life and then creating a daily structured rhythm, I created a plan to live by and I was more balanced. I had more clarity about my purposes, and I was more aligned in my daily life roles. Believe me when I say that without a plan, you will find yourself going round in circles and not gaining any forward momentum. You will not solve any of your problems.

What is needed is to build consistent energy into your life where you need it most – this is the primary purpose of Dawn Warrior. A personalised ritual was the game changer for my life and it can work for you, too. It will support you in developing strategies that will bring your life vision into reality, creating a lifestyle of constant forward motion, constant growth and expansion, and constant positive energy.

The first step is to consciously create the time and space to ask the deep questions, to listen for answers to discover what you really want, to discover what kind of seed is inside you that is longing to sprout forth and break into the light.

I know that you are curious about the transformational morning ritual that I'll be sharing in this book, but to maximise the power and potential of that ritual, it's crucial that we first take the time to ask ourselves three important questions in each area of our life. After that, I promise to reveal the details of the "Golden Hour" (as I call it), which changed my life – when you combine this morning ritual with the preparatory work of the following chapters, it will change your life, too. It might be tempting to leap ahead, but I promise you that your results will be deeper and more rewarding when you first set yourself up for success.

PART 2

DESIGN YOUR LIFE WITH THE FIVE Ps

One's destination is never a place, but rather a new way of looking at things.

Henry Miller

CHAPTER 6

THE THREE QUESTIONS

Have you ever really spent time looking at the course of your life? How did you get to where you are now? What were the main stepping stones? After you finished school or university, you probably landed that first job. Then you spent the next few years developing your career and your skills, buying a house with your partner, getting married and having kids – in whatever order it may have happened. *Fun fact: most people spend more time planning their annual holidays than they spend thinking about the patterns in their lives.*

That's because most people tend to follow a similar path to those around them, instead of actively delving – examining, exploring, questioning – what they really want and putting strategies in place to achieve it. The dreams and desires of men and women can become quashed by the stresses of early family life, and replaced by conflict and hurt feelings. If this situation twists further into bitterness and contempt, accusations and pain can be traded back and forth, and intimacy is in peril. It is important that new parents work together to hold onto their dreams, despite the challenges.

The three questions explained

The first and most powerful element of Dawn Warrior is a commitment to live consciously in all areas of your life. It invites mothers to take a brief pause for introspection and evaluation across each area of life, and I refer to these areas as the Five Ps:

1. **Physical** – health and fitness
2. **Psychological** – character, emotion and spirituality
3. **Partnerships** – love relationship and family and friends
4. **Parenting** – children
5. **Professional** – money and career

You will examine these areas in detail in the following chapters. Once you get clarity on what you want across all of these important dimensions, things get exciting. This is when the desire to grow up can also become a yearning to grow down. Your life changes in a fundamental way when you make conscious choices and create a plan to live those choices, not just daydream or wish for them.

Let's look at the three questions you will use to examine each area:

1. What do I believe?
2. What do I want and why do I want it?
3. What do I need to do to get it?

Now let's explore each of these a little more deeply...

1. *What do I believe?*

It is powerful to know what you believe and value. Your core belief about a life area, be it health or wealth, sets the tone and serves as a platform for all your actions related to that area.

THE THREE QUESTIONS

The Five Ps
Key Life Areas

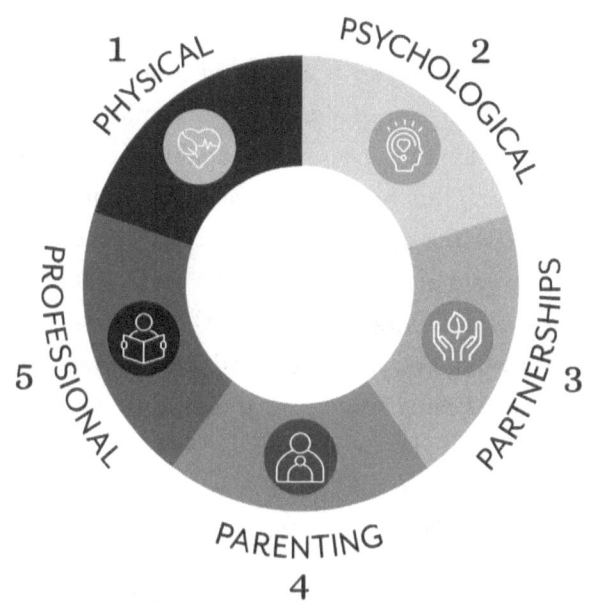

Much of what we believe and value has come from our training, our upbringing and the people around us instead of from our own conscious choices. By looking closely at them, you become aware of what those are. Do they empower you? Or are they just convenient or superficial ideas you adopted from others? You can't know until you ask the questions.

Getting clear about what you believe is important because your beliefs determine your thoughts and behaviour – and also control the level of your success. For example, confidence (believing in yourself and your capabilities) is a key factor for success in any endeavour, from raising a family and enjoying a high level of fitness to building a strong marriage or a great business. If you don't believe you are capable of developing skills or habits to reach those goals, you will find it difficult to follow through and take the daily steps required to get there. But once you become aware of what's holding you back – your self-doubt – you can develop a strategy (daily habit) to change that. I spent years believing that everything I did had to be perfect. Once two wonderful babies came into my life, this attitude caused me a lot of stress and I had to let go of that belief and develop a different mindset of resilience and flexibility, and greater trust in myself. That's what the Golden Hour is for!

2. What do I want & why do I want it?

When you investigate what it is that you want, and why, you'll discover your life vision. You'll realise the ideal state you want to achieve in each life area. Ask yourself: How do you want this area of your life to feel? What do you want it to look like? What do you want to be doing on a consistent basis? If your life was exactly how you want it to be in that life area, what would it consist of? Don't be afraid to set the bar high. Dream big.

The second half of this step involves asking, "Why?" Doing this will reveal the compelling reasons behind your desires. What energises you? What empowers you to take action? What motivates you to achieve your vision? Describe WHY you want to make the most out of this area of your life. More than any other single factor, why you want something will determine whether or not you achieve it. When your purpose is strong you'll do whatever it takes and overcome any obstacle to achieve your goal. One way to decide if you really want something is to ask yourself what you'll gain if you achieve it and what you'll lose if you don't.

3. *What do I need to do to get it?*

It's now that you will make a plan for how you will achieve your desires – you'll create goals and supporting habits. It refers to the specific actions that take you from where you are to where you want to be. How will you bring your vision into reality? Ask yourself what kind of positive habits, attitudes and action steps you can implement. What's the recipe for the vision you want to create in each area? In some cases, you might require the support of other people, such as a coach.

The key is to write down the steps you can take, no matter how small, which get you moving towards the achievement of your goals and living the life you want. This skill is not something we are born with and few schools teach it. Through practice, you will develop it, so go easy on yourself if you don't feel that you get the hang of it right from the start. Take it step-by-step and watch your little wins accumulate into major victories.

Everything is aligned

It is the target of Dawn Warrior to think deeply about each and every life area by asking ourselves the three questions that we have just explored. It is only then that we can develop the plan for our inspired life. When we take a step back and look at our answers to these questions, we realise that we not only have our overall life vision but the steps we must take to achieve it. When your life vision is aligned with your life goals AND with your daily habits, you are in alignment.

When I did this for the first time, I saw how everything was interconnected. And the reason why I have been so successful has to do with realising that interconnection. Your true journey in life begins once you know what your beliefs, goals and habits are – and you commit to them in every area of your life. So, are you ready? (Doing the work now of exploring the Five Ps will pay off hugely when you come to implement your new morning ritual!)

CHAPTER 7

P1 – PHYSICAL

The quality of our everyday living, and the extent of our lifespan, stems from having optimal health. It is the cornerstone of life. If our body is in physical alignment, our psychology has a better chance of being in alignment. And if our psychology is in alignment then our partnerships have a better chance of being in alignment, and so on.

Health and fitness is therefore the first step in the journey to creating the life of your dreams and becoming a Dawn Warrior. Your aim is to build your physical vibrancy while at the *same time* accepting your present state of health and fitness. This approach is important because many of us have struggled and failed to make lasting, positive change in this confusing and complex area of life. It's no wonder: we are bombarded daily with an overload of information that is often contradictory. So how are you going to figure out what is right for you?

The three questions

As a way to start creating a powerful and lasting change in your physical health, I recommend asking yourself the three questions from chapter 6:

1. What do I believe?
2. What do I want and why do I want it?
3. What do I need to do to get it?

Let's explore these...

Beliefs about health & fitness

There is so much noise in this area. We've all seen those many before-and-after images. Maybe we even tried the products on offer but didn't get the results that were promised. We've seen everything and we've tried everything to get the perfect body, only to experience failure and disappointment again and again. If you relate to this, I know where you're coming from, and I am happy to tell you that *there is another way*. The secret of Dawn Warrior is to find out who you are, deep down – before you try to change – to know what drives you and what kind of a person you really want to become.

All over the world, most cultures tend to share a common vision. There are some cultures where the norm is obesity. Australia is one of the fattest countries in the world right now so it's probably not a good idea to adopt our culture's vision. In many ways, the cards are stacked against us and if you make a commitment to optimal health you're definitely going to be disrupting the status quo. If we look around us, we see that our society currently produces a whole lot more sick, overweight and depressed people than it does healthy, happy ones. One of the biggest reasons is because our society is

P1 – PHYSICAL

wired to make people this way – there are some very powerful and wealthy special interests making billions of dollars. Obesity, cancer and depression may be the norm, but it's not normal – it's crazy. The health of our culture has been hijacked. We need to seriously consider opting out of that system and creating a better world for ourselves and our families. And it all starts by taking control of our vision for health and fitness.

Read through the following list of common beliefs about health and fitness and then take a few moments to record your own. (Yes, get out your pad and paper or open up your laptop!)

* "If I do weights it will make me huge."
* "I feel healthy so it's OK to put off my annual check-up until next year when I'll have more time."
* "If I exercise, I can drink and eat more and I won't gain weight."
* "I don't have time to worry about nutrition."
* "I've tried but I just can't lose my pregnancy weight."
* "I'll never be flexible enough to do yoga."
* "I tried vitamins but I just drag myself around all day with zero energy."

These are not only limiting beliefs; in most cases, they are based on false information. Remember, since your beliefs control your thoughts *and* behaviour, if you try to make changes in your health or fitness without changing your beliefs first, it's a recipe for failure and disappointment. That's why, especially in this area, it's essential to become aware of your negative beliefs before you move on to your goals. Otherwise, you'll just repeat the pattern and become even more discouraged.

The good news is that beliefs and values aren't fixed – we actually have the power to choose what we believe! So, looking at the list you've just written down, create several new beliefs that will empower and support you, such as:

- "I can make time for self-care."
- "My body is a gift, so I will love it for all the days we're together."
- "Nothing is more important than my physical health."
- "I am in control of my health and physical destiny."
- "My body is a blessing and wonder, full of energy and self-healing power."

Health & fitness goals

Take a few moments to consider what health and fitness mean to you – and don't forget the "why". Maybe you want to be stronger physically so you can dig that garden or lift both your kids with ease. Or you want to increase your heart health so you'll have more energy and sleep better. For many mums, fitness is important because it improves their intimacy with their partners, boosting their confidence and helping them feel more attractive.

Get very specific about what you want – ponder and delve deeply. Even if it sounds out of reach, write it down. Let yourself dream. Goal setting is the process of deciding what you want and planning how to get it. It's not something we are born with or learn in school. It's a skill and a step-by-step practice we develop over time, a practice in which our small wins become our major victories.

Years ago when I struggled with my weight, I decided to take a very basic common sense approach. I set a goal to study health and nutrition and learned what my metabolic type was. You see, everybody metabolises food differently and knowing your body type helps determine what kinds of foods are right for you, and what percentages of protein, carbs and healthy fats you need in your diet. Learning how to eat properly for my body type both in quantity and in quality of food literally changed my life. However, I'm not too strict about it; for instance, I allow myself to eat pasta every once in a while. But the key was learning what were the right foods for me. Be patient, knowing it may take a while. Remember, you can get professional help if you need it: consult a nutritionist, read a book or sign up for an online or audio program.

Strategies for peak health & fitness

Success will come when you start easy and be consistent. That's why you rely on your Golden Hour so that, at the minimum, you devote time to working out *every day*. Many people love yoga; some don't. Others are into running or swimming. You may find that the four-step program I've developed is ideal (see the Movement section in chapter 14). What's important is to experiment and try different things until you find the movement and activity that feels good and that you enjoy doing.

A new mum I'll call Michelle loved ballet but had given up the possibility of getting back into "ballet" shape – then she discovered some online classes that were ideal for her and she started doing a 20-minute barre class every day; eventually she worked up to an hour and a half and the joy she experienced brimmed over into her life and her family.

The secret to creating new habits

Positive change only results from the daily choices you make and the daily actions you take. Goals that don't change your behaviour are useless. Diets or fitness programs that don't change

GOLDEN HOUR AFFIRMATION

MY BODY IS ALWAYS BLOOMING AND RESHAPING AS MY SEASON IN LIFE CHANGES

#DAWNWARRIOR

your behaviour will not work. Research has shown that most programs, however, no matter how enthusiastically begun, usually fail to produce permanent positive results in people's lives. In other words, for the vast majority of people the changes don't stick. James Clear, in his brilliant book *Atomic Habits*, offers another way to change behaviour that is vastly more effective. He recommends giving up the struggle to change a habit; instead, change your identity. Build an identity that makes you rise above the habit altogether.

Let's say you decide to get a personal trainer with the goal of losing 5kg. But then you find that the membership isn't enough to keep you motivated, so instead of quitting you decide to focus on shifting to a new identity: you think of yourself as the person who goes to the gym regularly and loves it. Your new identity is: "I am a fit mother who goes to the gym three times a week, and I have the body of a sexy athlete". You will suddenly find that it becomes much easier because athletes don't skip workouts; it's not what they do.

These days, I love working out so much that it is a non-negotiable part of my morning ritual. But it wasn't always like that, and I know how tough it can be when you're starting out. Here are my favourite ways to fall in love with movement and get the most out of your workouts.

Work out from a place of love

It really doesn't matter what form of movement you are making, as long as you are having fun. By giving yourself permission to come from a place of love you can really tune in to what parts you enjoy and what parts are really a bore. Know that you don't have to slog it out all the time, and its OK to choose gentle, nurturing

GOLDEN HOUR AFFIRMATION

I AM LEANING DEEPER INTO
BEING A HEALTHY MAMA WHO IS
FULL OF ENERGY AND HAS
SELF-HEALING POWER

#DAWNWARRIOR

movements. Work out because you love the way it feels, and consider your mood and where you are in your cycle.

Connect with others

I love working out with others; you get to catch up and do a workout – so much goodness. However, when you're a mother, it can be hard to find somewhere that has a crèche or a timetable that works with your schedule. Instead, consider working out in a live online class, or organising monthly walks with a group (like I do!).

Gently push the comfort zone

I have a friend who has done the same classes for almost a decade and wonders why she doesn't get the results. Of course exercise is good, but your body likes diversity. It needs to be "surprised", and you can do this by varying your activities – this will also help you to keep growing. If you're like me and prefer slow change, gently push out of your comfort zone every week or so and see where it takes you.

> **Here is my personal "physical" mantra, to inspire you...**
>
> *I am in the best shape of my life, with abundant energy for myself, my work and my family.*
> *Being fit, slender and flexible is my physical identity.*
> *I eat clean, take vitamins, and exercise physically and mentally every day. I have a strong immune system, strong healing power, and a clear and calm mind.*

CHAPTER 8

P2 - PSYCHOLOGICAL

Living consciously is the foundation of this area. Most people live their lives blindly, without being aware of the values and beliefs that are shaping their thoughts and guiding their behaviour on a daily basis.

Thoughts become things

Whatever thoughts or beliefs you hold come into being *as your life*. If those thoughts or beliefs are negative, the result will always be negative. For example, if you believe that you are not a morning person, you will create every excuse and never actually get up early. The opposite is also true. For example, if you change your belief to be, "I am a morning person", you have shifted your identity. Suddenly you will start to do everything possible to get up early.

Exploring the nature of your psychological make-up is a wondrous thing. It will free you from living in survival mode, from going through your day being whipped around by every demand; instead, you will be *acting from a conscious intention*, which will empower you to achieve the life you desire and the one that is meant for you to live. You are here for a specific purpose, and in order to fulfil that purpose you must set aside ideas and behaviour you've learned that perhaps have nothing to do with who you really are!

Allow the desires and gifts deliberately placed within you to emerge. Don't minimise their power to guide, fulfil and transform your life. What is the universe seeking to create through you?

The three questions

"Psychological" relates to your inner self, so we will reflect on the three questions from chapter 6 when considering the elements that embody this area (your character, emotional states and spirituality):

1. What do I believe?
2. What do I want and why do I want it?
3. What do I need to do to get it?

Let's dive deep...

Beliefs about who you are

Starting with character: Who are you? What are you all about as a person? And what kind of person do you want to become? Your character is the sum total of your personality traits. It's your inner nature. This nature tends to determine your emotional nature – whether you are a person of high enthusiasm or reserve, whether you react with delight or frustration, or whether you remain calm in chaos or are easily flustered. It includes everything that embodies "you". Your behaviours, your thoughts, your ideas, your motives, your judgements, your temperament. All of these things go into shaping your identity.

When I reviewed my beliefs in this area and examined what it was that mattered to me, I realised that I valued truth and emotional intelligence. I wanted to live my truth – no more hiding, no more embellishing, no more being afraid to show vulnerability. I know who I am, and from now on, I resolved, it's the person I will reveal to the world. What supports this value is high emotional intelligence, which allows me to achieve excellence in every dimension of life. Emotional intelligence is made up of two components: insight and control. Emotional insight means being conscious of, accepting of and learning from my emotions. Emotional control is the ability to create the emotions I want in my life, and to let go of the ones I don't want.

Do you value honesty, kindness, emotional intelligence, fairness and respect? Almost everyone will answer a strong "yes". The quality of your character, however, depends on how deeply imprinted these values are onto your sense of self and to what extent they are revealed in your daily behaviour.

Some of the key questions to ask yourself are:

- Do you do the things you know you should do?
- Do you take care of your duties and responsibilities?
- Can you be counted on to make good decisions from a moral perspective?
- Do you do the things you know you shouldn't do?
- Do you find yourself able to justify lying, cheating or stealing?
- Above all, are you honest with yourself?

To be of strong character means knowing what you believe, what your values are, and living by those values consistently. We all have positive traits and negative traits. By taking an inventory of those traits, you can see how well equipped you are to live the life you want and be the person you want to be. Some traits, like impatience, can work in either direction. Impatience can hold us back, compelling us to act impulsively without a plan, or it can act as a useful kind of restlessness that moves forward with the energy we need to challenge the status quo.

To help you formulate your goals, take some time (at least 20 minutes and where you won't be interrupted) to make a list of your top five traits, with positive in one column and negative in the other. Be honest with yourself. You might even ask your friends or partner to help you – this will require a dose of that character-building quality of humility. Head to dawnwarrior.com/bookresources to access a worksheet that will help you to do this exercise.

Self-development goals

Most of us develop our personality and character traits by observing our parents and learning from our teachers and peers. They are learned.

We rarely question or consider changing them. *More often than not we are taught helplessness.* I can't because… "I'm poor", "I'm a minority" or "I'm a middle child". I can't because… "I'm not smart enough" or "I don't have the right background". If you hold onto these beliefs, you make yourself powerless. And, by the way, it is all completely untrue; the idea that there are lucky or chosen people is nonsense. It doesn't matter where you are in life. You have countless choices and what you choose will make all the difference.

One of the most empowering truths you can understand is this: you are in complete control of your life. You own it. You are in the driver's seat. If there is anything you don't like, if you are stressed or depressed, you have chosen it. Your choices got you there. And

GOLDEN HOUR AFFIRMATION

I DESERVE TO SEE THE SAME WARM GLOW IN MYSELF THAT I SEE IN OTHERS

#DAWNWARRIOR

the good news is: you can change almost anything about yourself if you become aware of your choices *and* if your desire to change is strong enough. Awareness and desire: these two traits empower you above all else.

I've discovered that having good character makes life flow. Living with integrity is far easier than living without integrity. My other goals are to develop kindness, compassion and respect for others. I will become a master at managing my emotional states. I will define and create the emotional states I want to feel on an ongoing basis.

So, what are the traits you want to have and practise on a daily basis? And why are they important to you? Take the time to ponder deeply and write down what emerges for you.

Habits: how will you get there?

Now that you have defined what qualities you want to have in your life and what they mean to you, your next step is to come up with habits to start living them.

As a mother, one of my personal goals is to experience consistent positive emotions like happiness, calmness and kindness. On a daily basis, I also use positive affirmations to release negative emotional states when they come up. For example, if I catch myself in a negative thought like, "There's no way I'm ever going to get this done today!" I counter it by saying something positive like, "I'm doing the best I can" or, "I'm a great mother".

Imagine what a trusted and loving friend would say – that is what you should be thinking to yourself when you hear that negative voice. The key is to be gentle *and* persistent and you will experience a shift in your thinking (that others will also notice). To make the change lasting, set up your day with the right intentions by working on your self-love affirmations in your Golden Hour time.

GOLDEN HOUR AFFIRMATION

I CHOOSE TO BE THE FULLEST EXPRESSION OF MYSELF NOW, AND TO CONTINUE TO FIND NEW WAYS TO BE SOFT WITH MYSELF

#DAWNWARRIOR

Mantras are profoundly powerful, and you'll find my personal mantras featured in the each of these "Five Ps" chapters – I hope that these inspire you. Use your affirmations and mantras as constant reminders to guide you back to your truth.

What is spirituality?

Another important factor that affects your character and emotional state is your spirituality. Let's begin by making an important distinction between religion and spirituality. Religion is a system of collective wisdom and beliefs containing rules and rituals. They address spiritual issues but they also address moral, social and cultural issues. We usually acquire religion as a belief system that's passed on to us from generation to generation, from family to family. Spirituality, however, cannot be handed down; it's developed by each individual.

Religion can give you the wisdom of the ages. It defines and it encourages certain beliefs that have been practised by entire cultures for centuries. It can point a whole society in the direction of living a moral life. But spirituality is not about cultures. It's not about societies. Rather, it's personal and goes directly to who and what you are at the deepest possible level: your relationship to the creator, the universe and "all that is". It concerns your purpose, and what you believe about why you're here. No one can hand you those answers. It's up to you to discover them for yourself. Your spirituality consists of your personal beliefs but it is also more than that; it's about the path you follow that unfolds in your life when you connect to that deep, spiritual place within yourself.

My spiritual journey is very much "à la carte", rather than "set menu". I am able to take certain practices that strike me as useful and apply them to my life in the moment, and I am also able to put practices that are less useful to one side. Although I was christened as an Anglican and attended a Uniting Church school, it was only years later in my adulthood that I started to follow the spiritual breadcrumbs of my curious heart.

It came about through a trip I took to Thailand in 2005, where I really took a liking to a couple of aspects of Thai culture. Upon my return, I enrolled in a course called *Overcoming Disturbing Emotions* at a local Buddhist centre. I did this to get a handle on the anger outbursts I was having (a well-kept secret), and I then enrolled in a beginners' course called *How to Meditate*. It was through these teachings that I began my ultimate self-development journey towards cultivating compassion and finding happiness in everyday life.

My brother gifted me with a mystical print of a woman and a lotus flower. This hangs proudly in my home, above where I carry out my morning practice. I've come to realise that, like the lotus, our destiny is a radiant future beyond anything we might presently conceive, and we must rise above the swamp to achieve the supreme bliss of oneness.

Plan for some time to consider and write down your spiritual beliefs. Also document how you view and experience your relationship to the universe. Do you see life as supporting you? Do you have a personal god? Or do you see the universe as an impersonal force? Many people regard nature as their primary spiritual connection. Is that true for you? How do you feel when you are connected to your spiritual centre?

What is your spiritual direction?

What direction do you see yourself going in, spiritually?

Exploring and strengthening your spirituality connects you to your purpose in a deeper way – beyond simply fulfilling responsibilities like paying your bills, taking care of your health, or even achieving your goals for home, work and family. This is because inner peace and calm do not come from, and have never come from, achievements, status or possessions. I'm not saying that these are not important; rather, spirituality draws us inward to the place where we can gain true knowledge of ourselves and tap into our power and our purpose. That's why inner peace is not a luxury; it's a necessity for a happy life.

My aim is to experience inner peace every day. Important to that sense of peace is my purpose of contributing to the peace of others and leaving this world a better place than I found it.

Here is my personal "psychological" mantra, to inspire you…

I experience happiness, calmness and deep belly laughs daily. I am aligned with my purpose. My distinctive qualities include integrity, kindness, compassion, and a knack for organisation.

CHAPTER 9

P3 – PARTNERSHIPS

Relationships are the most important and influential area of our lives. Numerous studies have shown that our emotional wellbeing, success, health and happiness are determined (for better or worse) by the quality of our relationships – the relationships we have with our romantic partner, our family and our friends. It's where the greatest satisfaction, and the greatest challenges, lies for us as humans. We are hard-wired to seek connections. Through relationships, we learn to give and receive, and to share our vulnerabilities and our strengths.

Your love relationship

Let's start by looking at romantic partnerships, arguably the most challenging type of partnership!

The three questions

Once again, you'll use the following questions from chapter 6:

1. What do I believe?

2. What do I want and why do I want it?
3. What do I need to do to get it?

Grab your journal, and let's get started...

Beliefs about love

Most of our beliefs about romantic relationships come from our family of origin and our friends. However, many people (unconsciously) hold highly negative and destructive ideas about love that they've received from popular myths and their reinforcement by movies, TV and the internet. Here are some myths to steer away from:

- "Men always lie, cheat and leave"
- "Women only care about money"
- "Men only care about sex"
- "I have to have a perfect body to attract the partner I want"
- "I'll never find the right partner"
- "Men aren't romantic"
- "Love relationships don't last"
- "Men won't talk about their feelings"

I'm sure you could add a few of your own to this list! If you hold any of these beliefs, it's "game over" before you even start. Not only are such negative expectations false, but they will also create the experience *you don't want*.

Vibrant and lasting love is not based on romantic feelings that come and go. Real love is based on our actions – actions that demonstrate deep caring for the person you love. These actions show genuine concern, empathy, compassion and trust. Most people want to be on the receiving end of these things but the average person isn't especially good at giving them. So, if you are committed to love, take a look at your ability to cultivate love *as an action*.

What are the beliefs that have been controlling your love life so far? Take time to ponder and write them down. Are there some that need to go? What will you replace them with? Be honest with yourself, because these values determine your experience – and if you happen to be currently without a partner, they will also affect who you are attracted to and who is attracted to you.

What do you want in a relationship?

Now's the time to choose what you want in your love relationship, and if you haven't been clear before, you can start over. Without specific goals in this area, your relationship is rudderless on a stormy sea. So go ahead and put it out there. Dare to have the relationship of your dreams. What are the qualities you want to experience on a consistent basis?

How do you rate the following: trust, mutual respect, reliability, kindness, openness, loyalty and, oh yeah, how about great sex?

Get clear with yourself, write it all down and consider what each goal will look like and feel like. For example, what does mutual respect feel like? How do you behave towards your partner when they are struggling or hurting? To be honest, after reading about Dr Gary Chapman's concept of the five love languages, my views on relationships shifted. My husband and I have been together for over 16 years, and I have learned so much from Dr Chapman's work. I now believe that we enter a partnership to inspire and support one another, to understand their preferred way of receiving love and to let them be the fullest expression of themselves.

GOLDEN HOUR AFFIRMATION

I EXPERIENCE A DEEP, CONNECTED AND INTIMATE RELATIONSHIP WITH MY PARTNER

#DAWNWARRIOR

Getting there

The first question here is, "What am I willing to do to make this relationship extraordinary?"

Communication is the lifeblood of any relationship, and the love relationship, in particular, requires effective communication in order to flourish. You have to be able to share honestly and openly. But it's not always easy to communicate your emotions with someone with whom you're in love because of the intensity of the feelings involved.

If your goal is to create a healthy, happy love relationship, the second question is: "Do you create an environment in which your partner can feel free to share feelings, thoughts, fantasies, hurts and complaints without the fear that you'll condemn, attack, lecture or simply withdraw?" If you can't answer "yes" to that question, and most couples can't, it's easy to see where the problems lie. Answering "yes" doesn't mean you agree with your partner – life just doesn't work that way – but it does mean that you both take responsibility for creating an atmosphere of trust, respect and acceptance; an atmosphere that allows you to express yourselves freely and with confidence that you will be heard.

Here are some communication strategies I've found to be exceptional for nurturing intimacy and respect, both of which are essential qualities for a fulfilling relationship.

1. **Pay attention to your partner**

    Simple awareness and acknowledgement of the other person is at the root of effective communication. This means that when you're dealing with the kids and your partner walks into the room, you stop – that is your man or woman, right there. You look up and make eye contact. Did they have a rough day? What do they need from you right now? Train your mind to tune in to and get connected with your mate. Learn to tap into that deep well of respect and appreciation instantly when your lover walks into the room. This habit alone, done consistently, will transform your relationship.

2. **Express appreciation constantly**

Don't let a single day go by without telling your lover how much you love and appreciate them. Choose a moment when you know it will land – when your partner is most receptive to hearing it. Also, be very specific. A general compliment has little impact and it's lazy. For example, to have the most impact, you might say something like, "Wow, honey, I noticed that you moved all those boxes and it made cleaning the garage so much easier".

3. **Learn how to handle disagreements intelligently**

When you encounter a disagreement, which you will, you have the opportunity to respond with emotional intelligence. When my husband and I are in the type of agitated emotional state where we can't think clearly and we kind of go crazy temporarily, we have an agreement whereby the first one who comes to their senses and apologises gets to be the hero.

Even when you're angry in the heat of the moment, try to remember that the person standing in front of you is your love, and you're on the same side – even when you disagree. You're there for each other, and your partner deserves the benefit of the doubt as often as possible. So be solution-oriented whenever you can, instead of lashing out.

If you can't bring compassion, understanding and empathy to the moment (and sometimes you just can't), perhaps give each other a little bit of distance, a little bit of space to cool down. But make it a race to apologise as soon as possible. This might take a few minutes, or an hour. Or it might be the next day, but when you're ready, say you're sorry and mean it. Make it a habit to take responsibility for your part because, let's face it, no conflict is completely one-sided.

4. **Go out on regular dates**

    My husband and I book a babysitter and go out once every two weeks. We take turns organising the dates, which means we only have to plan one date per month. We get dressed up to mark that it's an important occasion. However, the focus is on having fun, and doing what lights us up. These regular dates demonstrate our love and we so look forward to spending one-on-one time together.

The secret

The secret to a fantastic love relationship is commitment. Both partners need to be on board, and be willing and able to do what it takes. Commitment is the juice, the fuel, the oil that keeps the wheel moving. You can create a whole list of great strategies but without commitment, you will not be able to create a long-lasting nurturing relationship. Simple as that.

Here is my personal "love partnership" mantra, to inspire you…

> *Al and I are an amazing, unbreakable team. We are TAL – we Trust, Adore and Love each other deeply, passionately and respectfully.*

Your family & friends

Extended family and friends fulfil a different but essential dimension of our wellbeing. Once we marry and have children, our other relationships change, often because there is less time available to nourish them. Yet, most of us want and expect our family and close friends to share our joys and help us through our struggles. To see us. To understand us. To really know us. Like love relationships, however, most people rarely give thought to this transition and the ongoing care and focus that is required to maintain and nourish these life-long connections.

The three questions

Let's use the three questions from chapter 6 to chart your course in this area:

1. What do I believe?
2. What do I want and why do I want it?
3. What do I need to do to get it?

Beliefs about the role of family & friends

Family is our primary bond, and I believe that family should always be there for each other – through thick and thin. My parents, brother, sister, nieces and nephews occupy a very special place in my heart. Like most families, we have put a lot of effort into nurturing each other, but that doesn't mean that we don't fight and argue, because that's what family does. We help each other learn more about one another by holding up a mirror so that we can see ourselves through each other's eyes. We give each other a fresh perspective on who we are individually and collectively.

GOLDEN HOUR AFFIRMATION

I FREE MYSELF FROM COMPARISON AND MAKE SPACE FOR UNDERSTANDING AND FORGIVENESS

#DAWNWARRIOR

Creating fulfilling family relationships requires an investment of time and energy.

However, be aware of family relationships that are toxic and drain you. It is important to fiercely guard your energy and to put up a protection shield rather than succumb to the negative mood or emotional atmosphere around you. Sometimes removing yourself from situations isn't feasible, so a good question to ask is: "What changes do I need to make to make it healthy for me?"

Friendships are also essential to a full and happy life. Don't underestimate the power of your friends to absolutely turbocharge your quality of life. Creating and nurturing high-quality friendships can push your life forward faster and more powerfully than just about any other area. It's been said that your level of success will be the average of the five people with whom you spend the most time. A Harvard study found that people tend to become like their friends, so choose carefully. You will sink or you will rise to the level of the people with whom you surround yourself. Their values tend to rub off on you, for better or for worse.

Once you realise the importance of the quality of the relationships in your life, you can make a choice. Ask yourself whether or not your relationships inspire you and allow you to be the best version of yourself. Perhaps they are they causing you to shrink and become a modified version of yourself? Your answers will tell you a lot.

How do you view the role of family and friends in your life? Here are some questions to consider when assessing your beliefs and values:

- ✳ Do you have friendships that you treasure? What are their qualities?
- ✳ Do you allow yourself to gossip negatively about those close to you?

- Do you regularly reach out to check in or offer support?
- Do you reach out to friends or family only when you need them?
- Do you have friendships that drain you or feel out of balance?
- Do you fulfil just the "minimum" when it comes to maintaining connection?
- When a friend or family member asks for help, how do you respond?

What do you want?

Now that you have some clarity about your values and your behaviour towards your family (which reveals your true values), what do you actually want? When you take a similar inventory of your friendships, what desires and goals emerge?

The basis for a fulfilling relationship in this area, be it a close friend or family member, is a willingness to trust in each other, to communicate regularly (and effectively), to admit our mistakes and to take responsibility for our behaviour. It also helps if you maintain a sense of humour and humility.

I have a deep desire to experience wonder and adventure with those I love. This gives me a greater sense of wellbeing and ensures that collective life-long memories are made. My goals also include celebrating successes together, comforting each other in difficult times, and encouraging each other to become better versions of ourselves.

Having friends with a positive orientation in life is my most important goal. People with whom I share spiritual, emotional and professional growth. People who challenge me to be the best I can possibly be. Those are the people with whom I want to hang out because they are happy, healthy and empowering.

Take time now to set your goals in this area:

- Do you want to spend more quality time with your family?
- Are there some friendships you want to change or let go of?
- Do you want to add more fun activities to the time you spend with family or friends?
- Are there particular partnerships where you want to be more open or honest?

Getting there

Our intentions are important but, as always, it's our actions that will take us where we want to go. Once my husband and I became aware of the incredible importance of taking action, we put in place some powerful strategies. We set two goals to seriously improve our social life and we have never looked back. Firstly, we ceased contact with the people in our lives who drained our energy, and secondly, we consciously cultivated relationships that vastly improved our social life. And now, extraordinary friendships are the only types of friendships that we have.

When deciding on your goals, ask yourself, "What are the key factors in sustaining and growing my relationships with others?" Are you doing those things?

Here are some issues to consider that may help you set specific strategies for improving your relationships with family and friends:

- Time: When a relationship is working or feels right to us we can become complacent. Having a schedule of regular contact can help. For example, because we are so busy, my sister and I have a standing call every Sunday to make sure we stay connected.

* Collaboration: Among friends and families, there are often decisions or changes to be made that require discussion or consensus. It can be tempting to avoid approaching certain subjects or situations for fear of conflict, but openness and honesty will usually yield the best outcomes.

* Forgiveness: We all make mistakes, and it's important for the health and vitality of our relationships to ask for forgiveness and to show compassion, as well as tolerance, for the mistakes of others.

* Listening: This is the pillar of good relationships. When we actively listen, we are saying, "I am here for you" in a way that nothing else does. Darren J Gold says, "The greatest gift we can give someone is to truly listen to them".

Here is my personal "family and friends partnership" mantra, to inspire you...

I have extraordinary friendships that enhance my life. I love sharing my life's journey with my family and friends, and being mutually enriched, inspired and pulled forward towards my vision.

CHAPTER 10

P4 – PARENTING

Few people would refute the truism that no one can prepare you for parenting. When said at family gatherings, such a statement is likely to draw nods and loud sighs from mums who have the experience to prove it. We all know that taking classes, reading books and being in possession of the best parenting advice possible may expand our base of knowledge, but most of this flies into the wind on the day that a precious infant is placed in your arms.

As a parent, you are your child's world. You're the provider, you're the caregiver, you're the protector. You are everything. How you look at them, what you say – your every action is their example of what being a human is all about. They want to be you. If you are overweight, it doesn't matter what you say about junk food or sugar being unhealthy: you're giving them permission to be unhealthy every day. If you tell them to be kind and yet they witness your unkindness time after time, that's what they will learn.

However, your influence can also be positive.

GOLDEN HOUR AFFIRMATION

AS I WADE THROUGH THE EBBS AND FLOWS OF MAMAHOOD, I ALLOW MYSELF THE GRACE OF "STARTING OVER" WHENEVER I NEED TO

#DAWNWARRIOR

If you're someone who's not afraid to set goals and go after them, you're giving your child permission to be courageous. If you have a fantastic relationship with your partner, you're showing your children every day what a loving relationship looks like. The most important responsibility we have, as parents, is *to live the great lives that we would want for our children.*

Raising a child can be one of the richest, deepest and most rewarding experiences imaginable. It's an intellectual, emotional and spiritual journey that just can't be duplicated in any other way. It's also the most difficult, challenging and important job there is in life. Parenting is so important, in fact, that the entire human race depends on at least some of us doing it well.

Choosing consciousness

How good a job did your parents do? Did they raise you perfectly? What would you have changed? Have you ever thought to yourself, "I'm not going to raise my kids the way I was raised"? It's a cliché to blame our parents for everything we don't like about our lives. However, when we take an honest look back, we often realise that they were doing the best they could with the playbook they had. It's not very likely that they ever sat down and created a vision for their relationship with you or defined their parenting strategy clearly. Most parents don't bring a whole lot of consciousness to this process – however, it's different for us, because we have a tool that wasn't available to them and it's called Dawn Warrior. This tool is going to help you gain clarity for yourself as a parent and for your relationship with your children. You have a huge advantage.

The three questions

Consciously choosing your vision begins with the three questions from chapter 6:

1. What do I believe?
2. What do I want and why do I want it?
3. What do I need to do to get it?

These questions are important because you want to ensure that your children grow up happy and healthy and with the best chance of realising their purpose and potential in the world. It's a daunting order...

Beliefs about parenting

Let's start with the most basic question – "How do you see your role as parent?" Now, consider the values you believe are essential to instil in your children. Honesty? Tenacity? Respect? Compassion? Keep in mind all the while that it is your modelling of these traits that is the real teacher.

Fundamentally, my husband and I believe our job is to raise happy, healthy, independent and adventurous children. That's our mission as parents and it requires a safe, loving environment in which they can flourish. We protect and nourish our children psychologically by behaving rationally. We also do this by teaching them exactly what they need to know so they can navigate their way through life – beyond what schools, government and society teach.

To guide us on this path, my husband and I came up with a family north star. Pinned on our fridge, this acts as a gentle reminder of the values that we are committed to.

Family goals

What kind of family do you want to raise? What do you most want for your children? Happiness and health are common answers that parents give, but consider what that means, specifically.

The Hegerty Family North Star

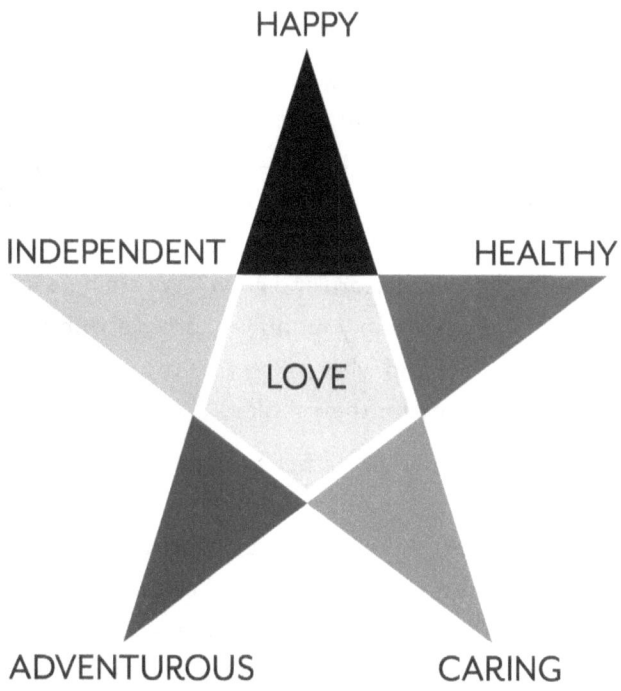

I believe that the primary mission of parents is to raise independent children. We want them to be able to function properly in our absence. This can be emotionally challenging because we don't want to let go. No parent does. It's difficult. But our job is to help our kids to develop and rely on *their own competence* to cope independently with the challenges of life. So, what is required? The freedom to make their own decisions.

To inspire you and give you a starting point, I'd like to share the parenting goals my husband Al and I have chosen. Our parenting style is to guide our children but to allow them to make their own choices, whenever possible and reasonable. This is important because the quality of their life experience is mostly going to depend on the decisions they make. If they struggle with a problem, we let them try to work it out because through struggles, we all learn and grow. "We are here for you," we say, "and we believe in your ability to cope with this". We set clear boundaries and when they cross the line they learn to take full responsibility for their choices.

We want our children to be healthy, and to understand that they have only one body and that it's got to last a lifetime. We want them to learn not only how to be physically fit, but how to keep their brain and mind emotionally healthy – to know their feelings are important, to learn how to pay attention to them and to seek to understand them. We want them to understand what a good relationship looks like and we do this by trying our best every day to set a good example.

We also want our kids to be happy and feel loved so there is plenty of kissing and hugging in our family. They also get a lot of praise when they achieve something and lots of encouragement when they don't. We surround them with as much love and positivity as we possibly can. We are only a kid once and we want them to be happy and enjoy the experience. And we don't want to push them too hard because life isn't a race or a stressful competition.

One of the goals we have for our children is to live life without fear. When our generation grew up, we played outside, fell out of trees, got cuts, broke our bones and came home when it got dark, and we were just fine. Keeping kids safe is a good thing and being cautious is important, but there is a difference between teaching kids to be safe and urging them to be afraid. Fear is one of the lucrative products that the media sells and when we start to view the world as a dangerous place, we put that on our children. The irony is that most of us live in a safe place, one where we don't have to worry about many of the real threats that humans have had to deal with – such as war and famine.

Love is another important goal – this refers to love for each other, but more importantly it refers to our children's love for themselves. Our family's number one goal is to encourage our kids to have positive beliefs about themselves.

Parenting expert Shelly Lefkoe has done some remarkable work in identifying negative beliefs that children have. The most common are: "I'm not good enough", "I'm powerless" and "I'm not important". Some of Shelly's solutions include: giving our children as much affection and love as we can; showing our kids attention by asking "what"-based questions not "why"-based questions; and acknowledging our children for who they are by telling them, "You are such a joy to be with" or, "I love being with you!" or, "You are so kind to your sibling". We sometimes put so much value on the actions that our children take, rather than valuing who they are as people – we are human beings, not human doings.

GOLDEN HOUR AFFIRMATION

I AM DOING MY BEST AND I
TRUST IN MY CHOICES

#DAWNWARRIOR

P4 – PARENTING

What are your habits?

When it comes to parenting, we all confront a large gap between what we desire and what we are capable of. It's essential that, in order to realise our goals, we confront and set aside whatever baggage we may carry from the past. What are the daily actions you can take that will ensure you can meet your parenting goals?

My husband and I have established simple principles that guide our parenting habits, and these principles are freedom, responsibility and love. When it comes to the concept of freedom, we believe that we do not own our kids; they own themselves. By modelling that we do not blame others, we teach our children to take responsibility for changing the way they act and behave. Lastly, and most importantly, is love. By exhibiting mutual love as a couple, children learn to become more kind and courteous and are less likely to violate the rights of others.

Kids change fast. So, naturally, as your children develop, goals and strategies will come and go. Every child is unique and has different strengths and needs and it's hard to keep up with them!

Do a deep dive for each of your children, and get specific. This is a two-step process:

1. Write a vivid brief description of your child (or children): who they are (personality and desires) and what stage of development they're in. What are their needs and what can you do to help them along their life path?

2. Define what is your relationship with your child at the moment. Where are you now as a parent and where would you like to be? What do you need to do to take them to the next level? For example, are you controlling them too much and need to loosen up and give them a bit more freedom, or are you too loose? How can you really help

them to blossom? Getting in touch with each child at this level can be a heart-warming and wonderful thing to do.

Every child in your life serves a divine purpose. They are here to enrich your heart, teach you something and provide a sacred opportunity for divine growth. And that's why you are here to serve them, too.

Here is my personal "parenting" mantra, to inspire you...

I spend time with my children, exploring nature and doing activities together that teach independence, respect and growth.

CHAPTER 11

P5 – PROFESSIONAL

The profession we pursue is an essential and large part of our life, not only because it's how we make the money we need to support our family and pay our bills, but also because it's a key part of our self-development and identity. The career we choose reflects who we are, and allows us to activate our potential and contribute to our community.

You're going to examine both "professional" elements – money and career – separately, and through the lens of the three questions from chapter 6 (the "What do I... ?" questions). This will help you to gain a full understanding of the choices and impact you can make in these key areas. Keep in mind that your career and your finances are deeply interconnected. One depends on the other. You can have a great career and have a completely messed-up financial life. You can also have a relatively modest career but manage your money well and create wealth for yourself.

Money

The belief that money is the root of all evil deeply permeates our society and represents a major emotional hurdle for a great many people. It's common to associate wealth with greed and selfishness. Rich people are often viewed with resentment, not only because of what they have but because it's assumed that to get rich you have to take advantage of other people.

Yet everybody wants to be wealthy. We read self-help books and take courses that proclaim, without apology, that having wealth is the gateway to freedom – and that we owe it to ourselves and our family to achieve financial success! Upon hearing that, we enthusiastically nod our heads and want to know how it's done.

Why does this love–hate relationship persist? Why do we continue to struggle with these conflicting messages, feelings and beliefs about money?

I believe it's because we were never taught the facts about money – what money is, how to make it, how to manage it. This important subject is not addressed throughout the course of standard Australian education. And the rest of the world doesn't do any better. We attend school for 15 or 20 years and we learn about everything *but* money. Then we graduate and we spend most of our waking hours for the rest of our lives trying to make money. The act of earning money takes so much of our time that we actually characterise it as what we do.

I know so many talented, disciplined, hardworking people who are completely dumbfounded when it comes to the subject of money. So it should be no surprise that we have serious money issues. Financial problems among couples are a leading cause of divorce. Lack of money is a leading cause of crime.

The three questions

I recommend bringing a warrior mindset to the close examination of your money life, and to ask yourself the three questions:

1. What do I believe?
2. What do I want and why do I want it?
3. What do I need to do to get it?

Take a deep breath, and dive right in – and be gentle with yourself throughout this process.

Get clear on your beliefs about money

Your beliefs and attitudes around money and wealth are going to have a major impact on whether (or not) you'll be able to create financial abundance in your life. How you think about money is definitely going to determine your financial condition. If you're confused or conflicted, it will show up in your behaviour and find its unfortunate way onto your financial balance sheet. That's why you need to choose consciously, and to decide for yourself what the value and function of money is going to be in your life.

I believe that financial abundance is available for anyone, that we are surrounded by opportunity and that there is no shortage of anything. Knowledge is power, and on our phones and computers we have all human knowledge available to us. I also view money as a tool – as a means and not as an end.

To my mind, it was crucial to drop all of the negative money beliefs that I learned growing up and to replace them with positive ones. For example:

* "The world is an abundant place" replaced "Money doesn't grow on trees"

* "Money allows me to create good in the world" replaced "Money is the root of all evil"

Consider the following questions to help you get clear on your money beliefs and values:

* What kind of relationship do you want with money?
* Why do you want more money in your life? What can it do for you?
* Do you deserve financial abundance? Do you believe it's possible to create it?
* How would your life change if you were fully on board with creating wealth?

Take a look at your spending habits. Is what you spend your money on aligned with your beliefs? Decide that, from now on, you will take a moment – before you whip out your wallet – to ensure that your potential purchases are aligned.

Your financial vision

People struggle to set financial goals (or are too fearful to set them) because they don't know how money works, or how to approach the building of wealth.

My husband and I have financial goals for our family and we also have our own individual business goals. Our aim is to be financially free in 10 years' time (via passive income and with no debt), to retire at an early age, and to provide our children with access to higher education if they want it. These goals support our financial vision, and I suggest that you create a financial vision before setting goals. A vision is greater than individual or family goals of financial solvency.

My life dream is founded on fostering a deep sense of connection and belonging that allows mothers to thrive, families to flourish and communities to rise. Don't be afraid to define a big vision, one that connects you to your deep desire and passion, one that holds meaning for you. The next step might be to learn about money and how it works: how wealth is built, how dreams are reached.

Habits: how will you do it?

Like anything else, wealth is the effect of specific actions. If you *do the things* that create wealth, you'll create wealth. If you don't, you won't. People become wealthy because they decide to become wealthy and then they do the things that wealthy people do. People stay poor because they have not yet decided to create financial abundance for themselves and they don't do the things that make it happen.

It's as simple as that.

When it comes to getting wealth, the first thought that comes to mind for most people is "I need to make more money". Of course, a bigger income will help. However, most people become wealthy by relying primarily on a solid, well-developed financial plan that creates long-term wealth, not just by making "more money" now, which is a short-term approach.

For example, my husband and I were both earning high incomes before I left my corporate career but it wasn't until we co-created a robust financial plan that we were able to forecast our future with certainty and confidence. The thing is, no matter how much you earn, if you don't have a plan and put in place habits, you will simply keep spending and won't get any closer to your goals. Our main priorities include giving our children the best start in life and having the necessary allowances to live the best quality life filled with travel, experiences, growth and learning.

GOLDEN HOUR AFFIRMATION

I RESPECT MONEY, AND MY WEALTH GROWS WITH EASE EVERY YEAR

#DAWNWARRIOR

Once you have a clear sense of your priorities and goals you'll probably need someone to help you develop your financial plan (unless you are dedicated, and great with money). Good financial planning reduces stress and ensures the realisation of your goals. It starts with getting a detailed picture of your cash flow: where's the money coming in and where's it going to? Once you've tracked your money flow, you have the information you need to create a budget, to forecast your short- and long-term needs, and to start a savings plan.

The great thing about having a plan is that once you get the ball rolling, habit implementation becomes automatic. At first, you may not see much difference. However, gradually, your efforts start to build. You notice your bank account growing. Your debts start to be paid off. It's a great feeling to watch this happen. What you've done is no less than lay a foundation that will support you and your family, for life – and provide the resources to realise your dreams.

Here is my personal "money" mantra, to inspire you...

Money enriches our lives and helps us enjoy all the things we want to do.

Career

Like most students preparing for university, I met with a career consultant to consider my options. What subject or field did I want to study? What was my career path going to be? The results of the session revealed that my passions included nature, organisation and the human body. As I reviewed the list of possible careers, sports science and events management stood out. You may remember me mentioning earlier that I started a sports science degree but soon realised it wasn't for me – once I pivoted into events management, I was very successful with it.

However, it wasn't until years later – when I discovered that purpose superseded passion – that I experienced meaning and true fulfilment in my work. *Purpose is the conviction that what you are doing matters.* It is even more fulfilling when you see that it is integrally connected to the wellbeing of others. When you can see the impact that your passionate efforts make, you feel motivated, excited and committed to your work on a whole new level.

Your career becomes more than a way to make an income or to follow an interest or passion. Most importantly, your work becomes less about your personal achievements (including money) and more about the life adventure you are capable of experiencing – and that you are helping others to experience.

What do you want to be when you grow up?

How many times were you asked this as a little kid? It may surprise you to know that it's a recent development in human history that people can even ask that question. In most ancient (and not-so-ancient) cultures, an individual had zero choices when it came to their occupation; they followed the same path as the family or village they were born into. But today we live in an age of limitless opportunities. Not only do we have a choice; we also have a wider range of choices than ever before. You can be a computer programmer, a flight attendant, an online marketer, an occupational therapist – one source I found listed 12,000 occupations!

Because of the thousands of professions that are available, it's natural to be overwhelmed. It can be bewildering and confusing to try to wrap your head around so many choices. How do you choose the right occupation? How do you know what's right for you?

This is where the critical consideration of your purpose comes into play. Naturally, you want to work in a field that interests you, that draws on your passions and talents. But if you want to experience a deep level of satisfaction and fulfilment, follow your purpose first. Purpose amplifies passion; it also directs it. Purpose leads you to consider what you want to *experience, grow into and contribute that lifts up and benefits your community and the world*.

The three questions

When considering the three questions as they relate to the area of your profession, view them through the lens of your purpose. (You might want to go back to Chapter 5 and review your answers to the "Begin with your purpose" exercise.)

1. What do I believe?
2. What do I want and why do I want it?
3. What do I need to do to get it?

Let's explore...

Beliefs: attitudes towards work & career

We learn about the world of work from our parents. If your dad or mum came home from work and regularly launched a tirade of complaints about their difficult day, you no doubt formed a distinctly negative idea about what it means to go out into the world and earn a living. On the other hand, if your parents demonstrated an enthusiasm for their profession, they probably imparted a desire (and a belief) that made you look forward to that phase of your life with eagerness and positivity.

The first step – regardless of where you are in the development of your career – is to look closely at the values you inherited or beliefs you formed about work and career. Here are some common attitudes that keep people from pursuing their dream career or from even considering work they would find fulfilling. Do you identify yourself in any of these?

* "Work is drudgery"
* "No matter how hard I work, I'll never have enough money"
* "I can't choose the career I really want"
* "It's smart to choose a secure profession like teaching or accounting, even if I'm not attracted to it"
* "I have a dream but I know it can't happen"
* "The day I'll be happy is the day I retire"

I grew up being encouraged by my family, and especially my grandfather, to choose a career that would develop my highest potential. He urged me to believe in myself and trust my capabilities. He often said, "Whatever you're drawn to, Tara, pursue it with all your heart and mind". His support and enthusiasm helped me to develop confidence.

Goals: where are you going?

Whether you work full time or part time, at home or away, it's an ongoing challenge to try to squeeze it all in. No one wants to spend the majority of their waking hours doing something they dislike. So, it makes good sense to pick something that you enjoy doing. If you fail to do that, you fail.

Maybe you feel trapped in an unsuitable career after having children. Or maybe you once had a dream of what you wanted to do, but life then got in the way. You found yourself stuck on a treadmill going nowhere and wondering what happened. It wasn't supposed to be like this, right? Eventually, you may have even accepted the situation as normal or inevitable, as many people do. The good

GOLDEN HOUR AFFIRMATION

I BELIEVE IN MY CREATIVE WORTH AND CHOOSE TO RISE UP IN A REWARDING CAREER

#DAWNWARRIOR

news is that you're not stuck; you have a choice – that's what being a Dawn Warrior is all about!

Not all of us have a career that involves directly creating wealth. Perhaps you're a stay-at-home mum, for instance. Running a household and raising little humans is a fantastic, amazing, super-important job. If you do parenting right, it means that you are also a nurse, a teacher, a housekeeper and a psychologist. Or, perhaps you're a mumpreneur. No matter your current career, it may be that you don't realise that your skills, experience and gifts could be shared with the world in a different way. It's important to honestly assess where you are now, to understand your true motivations for your career (be sure to take some time to do this where you won't be interrupted) and to be confident in your decision. And you're allowed to change your mind later if something interesting presents itself or if your circumstances change.

Maybe, right now, you are finding yourself doing a part-time "fill-in" job to help pay the bills. Maybe you're waiting for the day when your children are old enough so that you can get back to your full-time profession or finish university. Or maybe there's a program or certification you're interested in but right now you're so focused on your family and kids that you find yourself thinking, "Why bother? It's just too far off into the future".

If you were to imagine your ideal career, a career where you would have the opportunity to develop and use your full potential, what would it be? Is there a desire or field of interest you've tucked into the back of your mind (and heart) but have not allowed yourself to consider because it seems too impractical or unreasonable?

Write it down. (More than one? Write them all down!)

Habits: making it happen

Here are two key questions to guide you when developing effective career strategies:

1. How are you going to connect with your purpose, discover the work you are meant to do, and go on to make a conscious career choice?
2. How are you going to move towards your goals on a daily basis?

If you aren't where you want to be in your career right now, you don't have to make huge changes tomorrow. In fact, taking small *and* consistent steps is often more effective. You can approach this area gently, especially if you find it challenging. Just getting in touch with what you want (which you did in the goals exercise) will begin the process of positive change.

When I realised that I wanted to create a business, it seemed totally far-fetched, quite outside the realm of possibility. I was a mum with two little ones. But once I voiced my desire, it caught fire and I began to feel the power of purpose moving me through the apparent obstacles.

Creating strategies to achieve your goal involves breaking down everything into manageable pieces. Each task you complete boosts your confidence and creates momentum.

For example, let's say you love design and want to start a graphic design business. You have some previous experience and you've taken some courses but you realise that you need a degree or certification to attract clients. You've identified several online courses and the next step might be to do some research to compare their benefits and costs. After you select the top two or three programs, you can set up some information-gathering interviews with the director or people who've gone through the program. You'll want to dig behind the scenes of all the testimonial glitter before you make a commitment. And you'll need to determine how long the course will take you to complete and how much time you can give it on a daily or weekly basis.

Mama guilt

One demon you'll need to face is the guilt that comes with undertaking paid work. Or the guilt that comes with not working. Thoughts like:

- "I shouldn't be working – my kids need more attention."
- "I should be working so that we can afford more for the kids."
- "I didn't spend enough time playing with my child today."
- "I didn't get anything done because I was playing with my child."

The list goes on and on. Consider that perfectionism may be playing a role in creating your feelings of guilt. Are you being too hard on yourself? Trying to be everything to everyone? Sometimes guilt can serve as a signal that shows you're not living in alignment with your values. Those uncomfortable feelings may help you to pay closer attention to your life and motivate you to do things differently. Read: you are doing the best you can with what you have. Show yourself the compassion and love that you deserve and stop beating yourself up. You are doing much better than you think you are.

P5 – PROFESSIONAL

Here is my personal "career" mantra, to inspire you...

I love helping women to discover their purpose and reconnect with their passions. I feel appreciated by others and I know I make a serious difference to the success of every woman I work with.

The joy-filled climb

You have taken a close look at the Five Ps – **Physical, Psychological, Partnerships, Parenting** and **Professional** – and by doing so, you have thought deeply and consciously about all areas of your life. This is more than most people will ever do in their lifetime. You've also made a major step towards designing your future life, replacing the default beliefs and behaviours you learned from your family and your society with your own choices and attitudes.

Thinking about this stuff can be hard. It takes a lot of courage. You also need support along the way. Support from a joy-filled and high-achieving community of like-minded people is one of the keys to success that's often overlooked, especially when it seems as though you're looking up at the top of the mountain from the very base. (If you'd love to be part of a community of high-vibe modern mamas who will uplift and inspire you, I invite you to join *The Dawn Warrior Way* program – head to dawnwarrior.com/dawnwarrior way for details.) Don't do life and dreams alone – armour up!

Warriors do the things that are important, and potentially difficult. They also do these things regularly. Now that you have a blueprint for the creation of your most inspired life, your final step to living as a Dawn Warrior is implementation.

PART 3

BECOMING WHO YOU ARE

Remember that wherever your heart is, there you will find your treasure.

Paulo Coelho

CHAPTER 12

BRINGING YOUR PURPOSE INTO BEING

Loving yourself into taking even a single action, no matter how small, brings you to a new threshold. A bridge appears when you cross that threshold, but not before. The bridge is yours and yours alone. It is your destined path and the reason why you are on this earth. This purpose lives in your heart's core and longs to express through you and to become you. Dawn Warrior is here to give you the tools to bring your purpose into being.

The Dawn Warrior lives a life of purpose. She is not led by other people's choices or plans for her. She has awakened to her own.

This journey consists of four steps:

1. Create your life vision
2. Develop your plan
3. Take action every day
4. Measure and track your success

Following through on each of these steps will shave off years from your pursuit to be a better human, wife and mum. It will lead you to discover your own limitless potential and the awareness of how truly qualified and worthy you are to have an abundant life.

Create your life vision

This is your first step, and it's the beautiful moment when all of your hard work from part 2 pays off. The second question you asked yourself in each of the five life areas was, "What do I want and why do I want it?" Your answers now become your life goals. When you put all of these goals together they become your overall life vision! So take some time now and pull this together. Then take a minute to reflect on and appreciate what you have created.

You now have a target. All your actions should be directed at that target. This is the beauty of Dawn Warrior: you are no longer setting unrelated goals in a vacuum. Everything is connected. If you head to dawnwarrior.com/bookresources you'll gain access to my personal collection of goals from each life area, as well as my overall life vision. I hope that these inspire you!

Develop your plan

The direction of your life changes the instant you decide on a new goal. Goal setting is the process of deciding what you want. It is a skill you develop over time and improve through practice.

To activate your plan, follow these three steps:

1. **Define your foundational goals** – these are the five to six most important goals that make up your life vision
2. **Identify your overriding goal** – from your foundational goals, select the one that will drive success in all other areas

3. **Define your annual and quarterly goals** – to do this, look at your foundational goals, paying particular attention to your overriding goal (because this is the one that will make the biggest shift in your life). Break down these goals into what you want to achieve this year. Then consider what you need to achieve this quarter to ensure you that achieve your annual goals. When setting these shorter goals, refer back to the answers you wrote in reply to question three for each of the life areas – "What do I need to do to get it?" Those overall strategies give you the blueprint for the shorter-term goals you need to achieve to reach your life goals. The aim is to start every quarter with a solid set of goals that are linked to your annual goals, which came directly from your life vision.

Taking action

The Principle of Goal Synergy says that goal setting in line with a clear vision accelerates your results significantly. You are what you continuously do. Your habits define your days and your days define your life. If you can align those daily choices with your life vision and take purposeful, focused action every day towards your goals you'll reach that life vision. Guaranteed.

To ensure that you are taking the required actions, compile a list of daily actions or habits. The easiest way to do this is to take your quarterly goals and write down what action you consistently need to take to achieve them. For example, you could have a life goal of owning your own business, and this forms part of your life vision and is one of your foundational goals. Your annual goal in relation to this might be to complete a business course. Your quarterly goal might be to research and enrol in a business course. To achieve this quarterly goal your habit might be to spend 15 minutes each day researching, enquiring about curricula, and creating a shortlist of business courses. This is the power of the process, because you now have a daily action plan that directly relates back to your overall life vision.

Your plan of action is not enough

It's been said that our quality of life is created by the quality of our daily actions (including habits and routines). If a person is living a successful life, then she simply has in place the habits that create and sustain their success. However, there is a pitfall here that is often overlooked.

Many people connect with their purpose, create a plan and follow that plan. They work hard and expend a tremendous amount of energy, but never get anywhere. Their goal remains a goal that they don't achieve. They might be going down the wrong path for months or years but they don't know why.

What's happening here?

Taking daily actions is not enough unless you are *also* tracking and measuring the results of that action. Doing so will simplify things and keep you on track. It will ensure that you make tangible, measurable progress towards your overall life vision every day. If you don't do this, you have no way of knowing whether or not you're moving closer to your goal. Each little measurement provides feedback. It signals whether or not you are making progress or need to change course. Like an athlete tweaking their training regime, we, too, can improve our habits through trial and error. If one approach doesn't deliver the desired effect, we adjust.

Habit formation is a long race and as humans we need some immediate feedback that shows we are on the right path. This is where a habit tracker can help — my online program called *The Dawn Warrior Way*, which takes you deeper into the transformative work shared in this book, features a downloadable version that I use every day. (Head to dawnwarrior.com/dawnwarriorway for all of the program's details.)

Tracking your success

Measuring your progress is the single most important factor in maintaining constant momentum towards your life vision.

It's essential to track the following metrics:

1. **Your goals** — keep a record of your annual and quarterly goals and how you did. This is so that you can look back and track your performance (and adjust when necessary).
2. **Your habits** — track your daily habits so that you have a record of your performance every month
3. **Your life area scores every three months** — for this one you can use the Dawn Warrior self-assessment to see if all five life areas are in alignment (head to dawnwarrior.com/bookresources to download a self-assessment worksheet)

Review your goals and habits every quarter and assess how you did. Commit to starting now and doing this simple system for at least two quarters and see how it works for you. I bet you'll see massive improvements.

Accountability partner

Everything is difficult before it is easy. Every new experience is uncomfortable before it is comfortable. A key tool for breaking through your resistance is accountability, and there's no better way to receive this than to pair up with an accountability partner.

In the past, I've made a lot of commitments to myself about the direction I want to take my life. To be honest, I've failed many more times than I've succeeded. In the years of trial and error, I've found one constant: when I have someone to whom I am accountable, I am much more likely to stay on course and work harder on my goals.

So what is an accountability partner? It is someone you trust to hold you to the standards you set for yourself. This is a key point. An accountability partner does not set goals for you. However, she should be someone with whom you can discuss your goals and someone who will not judge you, especially when you fail. Instead, she will remind you of where you stand in your journey. Remember that failure is a pit stop on the road to progress, so if you're not failing, you're not setting your goals high enough.

The first two parts of this book have been all about understanding who you really are, designing a life that is true to you and fulfils your purposes, and then putting in place the goals and actions to get there. The next part of this book will show you how to become a Dawn Warrior. You'll discover how to tap into the power of the morning, and this will give you unlimited energy to make your life vision a reality.

CHAPTER 13

EMBRACE YOUR MORNINGS

One winter's morning at 4am, I woke to the familiar cry of my daughter. I struggled with having my sleep interrupted *again* due her silent reflux. "I shouldn't feel this way", I thought. "This is my child, and she needs me." I picked up my daughter and swayed back and forth, starting to hush her pain away. Her hair smelled of baby wash, and as her little body began to settle and snuggle into my chest, something happened. I inhaled deeply for what felt like the first time in months and was immediately struck by the fact that I was alive. The whole room took on a profound feeling of peace and I became fully present to the magic of the moment. The connection between us felt strong and secure as I took one step forward then swayed back on the other foot, each movement filled with intention and love.

I still remember being entranced when I watched mothers taking care of their babies, their faces sunken with worry and a million and one thoughts, exhausted and longing for relief and reprieve. I didn't want that to be me. Yet, I had fallen into a similar pattern...

until I discovered how to connect to and tap into a hidden level of energy and peace.

Your morning ritual

I discovered that rising at dawn – before other family members – gave me the opportunity to align with the energy of the new day. This energy is limitless. Through intention and the daily practise of my morning ritual, I began to draw from it steadily. By pouring energy into myself, I put on my Dawn Warrior before the Law of Entropy had a chance to subvert and steal away my day – the purpose for my day.

Also, there are real physical advantages to catching sunlight at dawn. We might think that vitamin D is the main benefit of sunlight, but the morning sun goes far further than just supplying this. Sunrise-light features more infrared light than regular daylight – and it contains little to no UV. Research shows that infrared light stimulates collagen, increases bone healing and preconditions our skin to protect us from the UVA and UVB light that comes out later in the day. Your eyes and your skin are your solar panels. Catch enough infrared light early in the morning and you are less likely to burn later in the day. Starting off your morning with a little sunshine vitamin not only helps you feel happier, it helps you sleep better, boosts metabolism, helps to improve the way your body absorbs nutrients, aids in regulating hormones and moods, and also boosts immune function. All these benefits come in as little as 10 to 20 minutes a day, with absolutely no cost to your bank account.

Creating a morning ritual that makes you feel awake, alert, physically and mentally healthy and ready to have an incredible day also offers you a hidden treasure and opportunity: the time to focus and work on your goals and dreams – dreams such as writing a book, starting a business or developing your art.

If the idea of being a "morning mama" just doesn't go down too well, I get it. Going from, "I'm not a morning mama" to, "I really want to become a morning mama" to, "I'm up early every morning, and it's amazing!" is a process. And if you're asking yourself, "How on earth can I get up earlier than I already do?", my answer is, "Don't be a broken mama". Choosing the path of a Dawn Warrior is not about denying yourself another hour of sleep so you can have an even longer, harder day. *It's about setting yourself up for success.*

I used to constantly battle with the thought, "Tomorrow I'll get up early". But when I changed the thought to, "Don't let my children's wake-up time be my wake-up time for the remainder of my life", things changed. When I made my own needs a priority, I noticed that I was able to give my full attention to my children. I was giving from a full cup, instead of an empty one. Build the habit now, and your future self will thank you.

Set the tone

Waking up in the morning, ready to roll, is your first challenge and it goes way beyond setting your alarm. The trick is to master the first five minutes by setting your intentions and making practical preparations the night before.

Have you ever noticed that the first thought you have in the morning is usually the last one you had when your head hit the pillow the night before? Think back to a night before a big event, such as a holiday or trip away. As soon as the alarm sounded, you opened your eyes, ready to jump out of bed and embrace the day. Why? Because the last thought you had was one of excitement. It also works the other way. If your last thought was something like, "I can't believe I have to get up in six hours – I'm going to be

GOLDEN HOUR AFFIRMATION

I AM LEANING DEEPER INTO BEING A MORNING MAMA WHO IS WORTHY OF "ME" TIME

#DAWNWARRIOR

exhausted!" then your first thought upon waking will likely be negative and full of dread.

The first step, then, is to consciously create a positive expectation at night for the next morning. For example, "I can't wait to work on my plan!" or, "Tomorrow I'm going to submit that proposal" (or finish that art project, spend time with my sister or husband, or have a meeting with a new supplier or virtual assistant etc).

Preparation is key

The way to have the kind of day you *want* is to plan for it. Since I know that the success of my morning starts the night before, I do things like packing school lunches, prepping breakfast and setting out clothes. Then I undertake the most important preparation: I make sure that I will get a good night's sleep. It can be so tempting to stay up late to catch up on the things I haven't done or just to have more time to myself; however, compromising on sleep puts me in a worse position the next day. Sleep improves your ability to think, allows you to have better moods and emotions throughout the day and helps your body to heal and recover.

I start by winding down my body and mind. Studies show that overstimulation is one of the main things that keeps us awake at night, so I limit my screen time and read instead. I have also experimented with sleep aids like magnesium supplements and blue-light-blocking glasses before bedtime. If I need more help to relax and let go of any stress, I treat myself to a sleep meditation and take time to reflect on the day. A side note: I learned that my red wine habit wasn't helping me. Alcohol helps you fall asleep, but you don't get the degree of true restful sleep your body requires.

Ariana Huffington is so devoted to good sleep that she's written a whole book about it – *The Sleep Revolution*. Here are some of her biggest takeaways:

* Experiment with sleep times until you know how many hours of sleep you need
* Determine the time you will need to turn out the lights based on the time you will need to be up the next morning
* Thirty minutes before you turn out the light, set an alarm that alerts you to "shutting-down time" – from that time on, computers, phones or TV are not allowed
* Create a before-bed routine to wind down – eg, have a bath and climb into bed with a book

So now you know how to get enough good-quality sleep, which will set you up for waking early and having plenty of energy for your day – but there might be a practical question that is crossing your mind. If you're going to be rising early, how do you refrain from waking up other people in the same room? A great idea is to use an alarm or watch that begins at a low volume and slowly increases in volume, or that has a vibrating feature. And if you feel adventurous, you might try something my grandfather taught me: the body's internal clock is just as good, if not better, than the contraption sounding on your bedside table. (Yes, it works!) As you're falling asleep, if you repeatedly tell yourself the time that you want to wake up, nine times out of 10 you will wake at that time. How? At the centre of your brain, a clump of nerves oversees your body's clock: the circadian rhythm. It controls your blood pressure, your body temperature and your sense of time. It turns your body into a finely tuned machine. That machine happens to love consistency. Your body is most efficient when there's a routine to follow. So if you hit the hay at the same time each night and awaken at the same time each morning, your body locks in that behaviour.

The ideal time to grab some "vitamin sunshine" is between 4.30am and 5.30am. However, it's best to check the dawn times in your area to ensure that you rise at the optimal time – this will mean that you really get to experience the benefits of waking up and enjoying the silence with no distractions.

Create a sacred space

You've probably heard the saying "home is where the heart is". This can be interpreted as meaning that home is wherever our loved ones are. However, it can also mean that home is a place where our hearts are filled with happiness, love and comfort. I encourage you to create a calm, nurturing retreat in your home. Setting up a place that's special and allows you time to relax, reflect and experience tranquillity can be a vital component of your morning ritual. *Tip: consider where this space would be in your house. Is it away from everyone else in the household so that you will be less likely to wake them up in the morning?*

It's a good idea to pick an area that has a lot of natural light. Studies have found that natural light coming through windows helps people to experience a stronger sense of wellbeing. Scientists believe that natural light helps the body stay aligned with its circadian rhythms. In turn, this helps regulate your energy levels when you are awake and asleep. Once you've designated a particular area in your home, get creative and set the tone by bringing to it items that have personal meaning. Think candles, ornaments, prints, music, crystals and a diffuser. Remember, too, that you can download your free *Warrior: One Morning at a Time* print from dawnwarrior.com/bookgift – have this printed and framed to display in your sacred space, and know that I am with you every morning.

Welcome your weekends

Oprah Winfrey says, "Waking up early on Saturday gives me an edge in finishing my work with a very relaxed mind. There is a feeling of time pressure on weekdays that aren't there on weekends. If I wake up early in the morning before anybody else, I can plan the day or at least my activities with a relaxed mind". I couldn't agree more with Oprah. I used to skip some early mornings, but it didn't take me long to realise that on the days when I got up and did my Golden Hour, I felt better, more fulfilled and more productive. I encourage you to experiment. See how you feel on the days when you skip your ritual. You may end up feeling, like many mamas do, that daily practise is better – and even if you are doing it every day you may just find that weekends are your favourite time to do it.

Your lifeline

This may sound completely counter-intuitive, but you don't have to do your ritual in the morning. Sometimes it's just not possible or convenient. Shift workers (like nurses) or new mothers often have schedules or lifestyles that simply don't allow them to create time in the morning. Choose what works for you – remembering that you need the time, you deserve the time, and you deserve the amazing benefits that result.

So what is this magic, you ask? Let me introduce you to my Golden Hour.

CHAPTER 14

THE GOLDEN HOUR

I have been practising my "Golden Hour" for some time now, and it's always been based on three elements. Using this framework faithfully has enabled me to set up my day and life for success and fulfilment, instead of failure and frustration. And that's when my friends and associates started commenting on my natural positivity, and how good it made them feel to be in my company. As your life energy expands and strengthens as a result of giving yourself the gift of a Golden Hour, others will also notice and be attracted to the change taking place inside of you.

Three elements

I developed the Golden Hour method from a place of curiosity and love, and it features three elements. Depending on your personal circumstances, the activities you focus on within each element will differ, and so will the time you may choose to spend on each one. However, the *combination* of elements gives modern mamas the key to self-renewal and the personal growth needed to thrive in life.

The Golden Hour includes these three essential elements:

1. **Movement** – working "out" in a way that is good for me
2. **Mindset** – working "in" in a way that is good for me
3. **Magic** – working "on" tasks that are aligned with me

1. Movement

The first element is **movement**, which helps your brain to wake up completely. Do whatever activity you like – yoga, Pilates or low-intensity exercise – but you must sweat a little. Cortisol is a hormone of stress, which is caused by fear. Exercise will lower your cortisol and release BNDF (brain-derived neurotrophic factor), which reduces stress. You'll not only become stronger and more energetic, but you'll also sharpen your focus. As a bonus, research shows that morning exercise helps our bodies break down sugar and burn fat.

I tailor this component according to my mood, energy levels and cycle. It turns out that tailoring your workouts to your cycle – a technique known as phase-based training – empowers you to look, feel and perform your best. Georgie Bruinvels, PhD, a co-creator of the FitrWoman App, says, "The way you move and breathe, how your heart beats, and your body's reaction to exercise varies throughout your menstrual cycle". So by getting to know my cycle and how it impacts my body (and why on some days exercise feels like a chore), I tweak my workouts accordingly.

Make your own movement routine and try out different kinds of exercise until you discover what works best for you. I have a couple of suggestions for you; however, feel free to adapt them or, as suggested, create your own. My all-time favourite is a Kundalini yoga

The Golden Hour

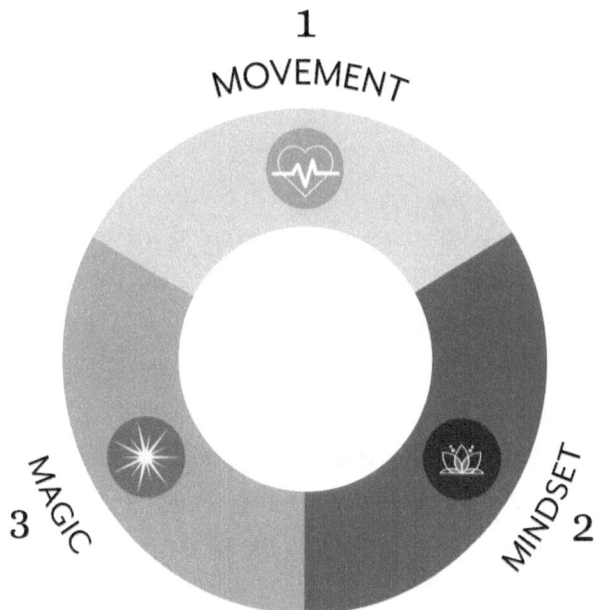

kriya, followed by a short high-intensity Tabata. Another is a four-step workout inspired by Ben Greenfield Fitness that incorporates mind, body and spirit (I outline the steps in this workout below). The strength, movement and breathwork involved in my morning workouts are just enough to jump-start my body.

1. **Intention** – I take three deep belly breaths through the nose and out of the mouth. On the final breath, I think of a clear and specific word or phrase I want to align myself with, like "strength", "focus" or "compassion for myself and others". I breathe the intention into my heart with three additional deep breaths.

2. **Breathwork** – I am a huge fan of Kundalini breathwork for turning on the body, mind and spirit, warming the muscles and charging the body with *ki* (life force). I arrange this portion of the workout with yoga sun salutations and Kundalini fire breathing (rapid, sharp, deep inhales followed by short, shallow exhales, preferably all through the nose).

3. **Callisthenics** – these exercises make the body slightly anaerobic. Exercises include alternate lunge jumps, burpees or sitting down and standing up fast as possible (deceptively difficult).

4. **Strength** – this includes 10 super-slow squats plus a one-minute squat hold. Then I complete squat jumps, and undertake another round from the start but with push-ups. Then I finish with 30 seconds of deep nasal breathing before performing my meditation.

2. Mindset

The second Golden Hour element is **mindset**, which helps to cultivate the "whole person". Our brain is a wonderful organ that has the ability to learn new skills, integrate new experiences and store memories. Stimulating the mind has been shown to improve brain function and promote the formation of new neural circuits. The most powerful method (and the one I prefer) to improve our mindset is **meditation**. What is really cool about meditation is that it can help slow your brainwaves down into a state where you stop worrying – something every mother will appreciate.

The power of meditation lies in the relaxation response, which is the opposite of the fight-or-flight response. Dr Herbert Benson, a pioneer of mind–body research, describes the relaxation response as, "a physical state of deep relaxation which engages the parasympathetic nervous system". This changes the beta waves of stress into alpha waves of peace. **In short, meditation is a point-blank defence against stress and burnout.**

Meditation is a practice of awareness that has helped many mothers I've worked with. You sit and be present with yourself, the self that you ARE right now. You do not need to "switch off" your brain. Just allow yourself to be present and be aware of your thoughts and feelings. Once awareness rises, so does wisdom and creativity, and these are extremely powerful and transformational. My suggestion is to start by using guided meditations as they will help to ease the transition from a busy mind to a quiet mind. I have created guided meditations and shared them on Spotify and Insight Timer – they vary in length from a couple of minutes to 10 or so minutes. Head to dawnwarrior.com/bookresources to gain access to the link. However, for busy mums of infants and young children, movement meditation is a great substitute.

There are other effective methods for shifting out of stress into the relaxation response, and these include visualisation, progressive muscle relaxation, energy healing, chakra balancing, acupuncture, massage, breathing techniques, mindfulness, journaling, prayer affirmations, mantras or chanting, tai chi, qi gong and yoga. Participating in these kinds of activities focuses our mind on the present moment so that we can enter and hang out in the relaxation response. While we are in this state our bodies are experiencing peak performance: our digestive systems are operating correctly; our immune system is functioning at full capacity; and the neurochemicals that are being circulated through our bodies are providing a healthy, balanced environment for our cells to grow and reproduce.

To help positively re-program your mind, I especially recommend using Golden Hour Affirmations. You'll have seen these as you've made your way through this book. They have been written from my heart, with intention (although you can always use them as inspiration for the writing of your own), and by saying them constantly you'll start to change your world in a powerful way.

The study of spiritual teachings from the ancient traditions of Hindu, Buddhist and Taoist philosophy have also helped me to understand and use the mind, and to explore the depths of consciousness present within each one of us. The most important teaching is embodied in this quote:

> *The thought manifests as the word;*
> *The word manifests as the deed;*
> *The deed develops into habit;*
> *And habit hardens into character;*
> *So watch the thought and its ways with care,*
> *and let it spring from love born out of concern*
> *for all beings...*
> *As the shadow follows the body,*
> *as we think so we become.*

3. Magic

The third element of the Golden Hour is **magic**. This is when everything in the Dawn Warrior process really comes together – and it really is magical! During this time, you take inspired action that moves you towards your life vision. You start by spending the first few minutes reflecting on and tracking the list of daily habits that you created in Part 2 of this book. Here is a question you can ask yourself every day to keep you on track: "Did I implement the habit or not?"

Next, you actively work on your current life goals in real time. The steps to uncover your goals are in the "Develop Your Plan" part of this book in chapter 12, where you identified a solid set of goals that are linked to your annual goals, which came directly from your life vision. There is enormous power in putting your Golden Hour to use on your most creative and fulfilling projects. You will find yourself making large strides on goals that would otherwise have sat on the backburner, and you will feel a sense of productivity that you can then take with you into the rest of your day.

One mother's story

One mother I worked with had a life vision that involved changing her career and switching industries to help children with special needs. She used this time in her morning ritual to research what credentials she needed, how long it would take to complete the studies, and whether this could work as part of her current lifestyle. She even arranged to meet a local school and see first-hand what it would be like to work in this industry before committing to taking the next step.

She used the powerful tool of journaling to help her explore how this new career might look in her life and really reflected on whether this was the right step for her. She soon had a list of annual, quarterly and weekly goals she wanted to achieve to make the transition, and a list of daily habits to support the career (and identity) change that she was shifting into. This was all completed in her Golden Hour, uninterrupted and in her own sacred time.

She shares, "Even though I'm making small steps toward my vision, I still feel like I'm moving forward in my life and working towards something meaningful to me. It truly makes me want to get out of bed every day. It gives me this burst of energy I never had before. And I really notice on the days when I don't get up and make it happen".

Why it works

One of the main reasons why the Golden Hour method is so effective is that it uses the feminine and masculine energies that we all have. I encourage you to welcome and be intentional about fostering a balancing act of these energies within yourself.

Masculine energy is characterised by doing and achieving and is moulded by logic and reason, apparent in such activities as analytical thinking, business planning and creating structure. The feminine complement to this is intuitive, oriented to receiving and allowing, and characterised by being. It is natural for those with a business background to draw primarily from their masculine energy and be action-oriented, with a strong tendency to suppress their feminine energy. When we open up to our mindset and intuition, however, and allow the gentle, receiving energy to pour in, we come into a new balance – and our true power. To be successful, we need to integrate both of these into our daily lives.

Using your intuition (feminine) AND your analytical mind (masculine) harmoniously in the Golden Hour is key to true inner union. You cannot really separate them at all. It's like yin and yang. They work together. By combining both aspects, you will not only have a sense of accomplishment but a feeling of balance from within.

More than just a morning ritual

As you can see, the Golden Hour goes beyond being just a morning ritual. It is your inspired life all wrapped up in a big ball of actionable magic. It is a process that involves understanding who you are, what you would like your life to look like and what goals and habits will get you there, and carving out the time in your morning ritual to track, reflect and act on these. In other words, it is a practice, a tool and a commitment to make your dreams become a reality, one morning at a time!

A tip about interruptions... They may happen frequently, but these are the moments that I embrace the most. They are gentle reminders that life ebbs and flows and so must we. My meditation may start as one thing, but if I'm interrupted it can turn into a movement meditation with the kids. The beautiful beats of the music, the swaying of the bodies and the visions of connecting to mother earth are just as enjoyable as those meditations where I am sitting down and am in a trance. And I know that things are OK when I find my three-year-old son sitting on a couch, looking out of the window. When asked, "What are you doing?" he replies, "Just meditating".

I want to leave you with the secret to success: accomplishing your goals and creating the life you want does not come from the days, weeks or months of prescriptive practices. Yes, meditation, journaling, calisthenics, gratitude lists, physical disciplines of yoga, tai chi etc are all amazing and effective. But the Golden Hour is more than a set of disciplines; it's about tuning into and receiving the signals our body has for us. So where before it was, "I am going to do yoga and it looks this way but I don't really feel like that today", it is now, "I'll just keep doing it until I get into the flow of it" or, "When I do this part, it's amazing, but the rest feels like a chore" it becomes, "I'm going to put aside those bits that aren't my joy and pursue the bits that are". Those perspective shifts that allow you to set an intention but adjust according to the moment will lead you to the next thing that brings you joy, and the next. By tapping into your own experience and "fun feedback", your body and soul are guiding you to move towards your own happiness, which you can then share with others.

CHAPTER 15

ON LOVING YOURSELF

Without exception, the key to success in every aspect of your life is loving yourself. If you don't love yourself, why would you deem yourself worthy of pursuing your purpose? If you don't love yourself, how will you be able to see the value in yourself and in what you have to offer the world? It's everything.

When I was younger, I tried very diligently (like most young women) to fit into the world around me. I constantly adjusted my language, my clothing, my mannerisms and my behaviour to avoid doing anything that might make me look foolish. In my desperate attempts to fit in, I lost myself. I stifled my true nature – I was so afraid to stand out that I shrank in order to fit in.

Another terrible thing happened. I developed the habit of excessive and harsh self-criticism. I said things to myself that I would never say to anyone else. I judged myself for not being confident. I criticised my appearance; I mentally noted all of the areas of my body that needed toning and slimming. I pinched my sides, the backs of my arms, and my thighs, reminding myself of how much work I had to do. I mentally took note of how my clothes fit, how my body felt, how I wanted to look and feel and on and on. This obsession over my physical appearance started in school and through the years grew to a dangerous level. I was letting my inner critic speak to me poorly.

The Dawn Warrior process built my confidence and self-love. Little by little, I started doing things that made me feel good, and I stopped doing the things that made me contract and feel small. I did this by implementing daily habits and practices, and by using audio courses, meditation, affirmations and countless self-help books. There came a point, one afternoon when I was developing my goals for the New Year, when I realised I had made the shift. The critical voice no longer ruled me. In its place was unconditional love for myself.

Forging a Dawn Warrior mindset

It all started with a decision to consciously change my internal dialogue. At first, I had to take it minute by minute. When an internal negative voice jumped out at me, like "You're so stupid! I can't believe you just said [or did] that!" I intentionally shifted my critical internal voice to say, "But I'm choosing to love myself anyway". Many times my mental shift wasn't enough. The negative voice would continue, so I had to go deeper and make the emotional shift. Two important tools helped me do this: a daily gratitude list and writing affirmations.

Slowly, the affirmations I was rehearsing over and over started to take root and change my beliefs and values – and my behaviour. I started to feel the love I was showing myself and I started to believe it. Of course, I still have moments when I fall into negative self-talk but today I can catch it quickly and shift immediately. Here are some of the affirmations that have worked for me (and keep an eye out for the Golden Hour Affirmations scattered throughout this book, as well as my own personal mama mantras, which I use regularly and have honed over time – I hope these inspire you to create your own):

- ✷ I love and accept myself exactly as I am
- ✷ My body is healthy; my mind is brilliant; my soul is tranquil
- ✷ My relationship with my husband and children is strong, deep and loving
- ✷ My business is growing, expanding and thriving
- ✷ Creative energy runs through me and leads me to new and brilliant ideas

This method also helped me overcome my eating disorder. Without even realising it, when I was younger I developed an unhealthy eating habit. For many years, whenever I was stressed or upset I would binge on food in order to self-soothe. And the quickest and easiest foods were the first things I went for. I very rarely do this now, but it took years of rewiring my brain through my daily habits to change this behaviour.

My self-sabotaging gradually stopped. I began to forge a Dawn Warrior mindset, which freed me to think and act *for* myself instead of against myself. This new mindset expanded my consciousness to the point where I was able to see possibilities that were no longer vain hopes or daydreams. I knew my vision and my goals were within my grasp.

You are unique

Another powerful key to loving yourself is to realise and appreciate your uniqueness. This is a game changer. Consider this: several billion people have walked the earth, but there has never been, nor will there ever be, a person exactly like you. Your uniqueness gives you real value. You are special and are gifted specifically for a purpose that only you can accomplish. You are wonderfully made. Saint and philosopher Augustine wrote in AD 399, "Man travels hundreds of miles to gaze at the broad expanse of the oceans. He looks in awe at the heavens above. He stares in wonderment at the fields, the mountains, the rivers and the streams. And then he passes himself by without a thought... the most amazing creation".

The power of mindset

Mindset is largely something that we adopt without conscious thought – it occurs at a subconscious level, based on how we've been programmed to think, believe and act. Our programming comes from many influences, including what others tell us, what we tell ourselves, and the sum of our positive and negative experiences. It starts early by imitating and trying to please our parents and then it extends to our siblings, peers, colleagues, friends, spouse and, yes, children. At some point, most of us realise that this programming is interfering with our goals or with our desire to just relax and be ourselves. So we begin by challenging it and undertaking the necessary job of changing it.

Affirmations are a tool for making this change. They enable you to become more intentional about your goals while also providing the encouragement and positive mindset necessary to achieve them. When you repeatedly tell yourself who you want to be, what you want to accomplish and how you are going to achieve it, your subconscious mind will shift your beliefs and behaviour. Once you believe and act in new ways, you will begin to manifest your affirmations into reality. Science has proven that affirmations – when done correctly – are one of the most effective tools for quickly becoming the person you need to be to achieve everything you want in your life: for yourself and your children. And yet, affirmations also get a bad rap.

Many people have tried them, only to be disappointed because they see little or no results. Why? Countless so-called experts have taught affirmations in ways that have proven to be ineffective and set up people for failure. There are two common problems with affirmations.

The first is lying to yourself. Saying things like, "I am the best parent in the world" or, "I have achieved all of my goals this year". Nope, sorry, you haven't. Creating affirmations as if you've already become or achieved something is probably the single biggest reason that affirmations don't work for most people. With this approach, every time you recite the affirmation that isn't rooted in truth, your subconscious resists it. As an intelligent human being who isn't delusional, lying to yourself repeatedly will never be an optimum strategy. The truth will always prevail.

The second problem is the use of passive language. Many affirmations are designed to make you feel good by creating an empty promise of something you desire. For example, here is a popular money affirmation that's been perpetuated by many world-famous gurus: "I am a money magnet. Money flows to me effortlessly and in abundance". This type of affirmation might make you feel good in the moment by giving you a false sense of relief from your financial worries, but it won't generate any income. People who sit back and wait for money to show up magically are cash poor. To generate the kind of abundance you want (or any result you desire), *you've got to actually do something.*

If affirmations aren't your "thing", consider turning them into questions. For example, by simply turning the affirmation statement of, "I am an incredibly loving mother" into a question – such

GOLDEN HOUR AFFIRMATION

I AM BRAVE ENOUGH
TO SEE MYSELF, EVEN WHEN
OTHERS DON'T

#DAWNWARRIOR

ON LOVING YOURSELF

as, "Why am I such an incredibly loving mother?" – your brain starts searching for the answers instead of battling the statement.

I often use affirmations during my meditation as part of my Golden Hour. The lower-frequency brain waves experienced during meditation actually help to implant the affirmations into our subconscious.

True self-esteem is born out of our actions. Your actions must be in alignment with your desired results, and your affirmations must articulate and affirm both.

What action will you take today?

CHAPTER 16

LIVING YOUR VISION

When we live consciously, our vision bears fruit and our purpose becomes manifested. Day by day, seeing and feeling your vision come alive is one of the most fulfilling and amazing experiences you will have. The skills you develop, the wealth you achieve, the contribution you make to your community... all lift you to a new plane. And we experience joy when we realise that we are no longer held captive by old beliefs telling us we were not smart enough, talented enough or good enough – or that our goals were impossible to achieve. All of this is washed away. Insecurity grows into confidence in our capabilities; self-doubt and fear become faith in our gifts and our purpose.

The journey of consciousness

Even more amazing than vision manifestation is the awareness that you are travelling a road of ever-increasing consciousness.

At each level, we expand into experiencing a greater sense of harmony until we become fully aligned with our world, both internally and externally.

Level 1: Life happens to you

Many of us start here, not realising that we're playing the victim role. When our goals fall flat, we say, "Why is this happening to me?" or, "It's just my luck these that things happened to me". At this stage, it's easy to blame other people and circumstances because you have not yet taken responsibility for making your life what it is.

Level 2: Life happens by me

You have moved into the driver's seat, realising that you don't have to be a victim of circumstances and remain stuck in old beliefs anymore. You're empowered and free and it feels so good! The challenge at this level is that you can become obsessed with taking action and get trapped in the "doing" mode – resulting in your life becoming unbalanced, and exhausting.

Level 3: Life happens through me

You are no longer taking action all the time; you've learned to carve out the essential time to just BE, without an agenda. You allow yourself to do whatever it is that raises your vibes. That's why I spend so much of my Golden Hour on energy-raising activities like meditation, journaling and yoga. When you move into the third level of conscious living, life happens in you and for you and through you. This is where the magic happens, and it's incredible.

When life happens in you, you start to notice life's coincidences. For instance, someone comes into your life just when you need them or a door opens and the perfect opportunity lands in your lap.

For example, when I feel like I want to connect with someone I haven't spoken to in a while, they often contact me within a few days. It's as though they are picking up on my energy to connect. When these connections happen or an incident happens in my favour, I feel aligned and I find myself thanking the universe.

The more you pay attention to the magic, the more the universe will invite you to new horizons. That's because the universe wants to guide us; it wants to give us little breadcrumbs to follow. Most of the time, people are the conduits for the messages and guidance we need.

Living in true alignment

When you have a set plan and you are ploughing ahead, it can often feel as though you're paddling upstream. It's hard work. When your efforts feel like that, you are probably in the "life happens by me" mode. You need to turn around your boat, release the oars a bit and allow life to just flow through you. When you do this, pursuing your vision becomes a lot easier.

When you're fixated on a goal, it's easy to get locked into a rigid perspective that doesn't allow new ideas or approaches to come to you. That's the time to open to the bigger picture at play – where life is happening *for* you and not *to* you. By just pausing, you can create an opening for the universe to guide you to where you need to be. This is living in true alignment.

Eight Dawn Warrior principles

Our daily practices and actions are specific to our vision, but our principles are deep, internal truths that direct us through life. It is at the level of principles that we become rooted in our purpose. It is from principles that the changes we make are lasting, changes that can create a legacy beyond our own lifetime.

Stephen Covey writes, "Correct principles are like compasses: they are always pointing the way. And if we know how to read them, we won't get lost, confused, or fooled by conflicting voices and values".

Principles keep us on track, even when our goals change, or when we hit a place in life where we have to re-calibrate and heal before going forward. What a powerful piece of teaching this is.

These are the Dawn Warrior principles that I encourage you to read regularly and take into your heart:

1. **The Principle of Self-Responsibility**

    Your life is yours. You own it. You are in the driver's seat.

2. **The Principle of Cause and Effect**

    Your life is a result of your daily choices and actions. Your choices and actions are the cause, and the quality of your life is the effect.

3. **The Principle of Effective Implementation**

    This principle consists of four connected steps:

    1. Get clear on your vision
    2. Develop your plan
    3. Take action every day
    4. Measure and report your progress

4. **The Principle of Infinite Variables**

    No plan, no matter how well developed, can take into consideration the infinite variables you'll encounter when you put your plan into action in the real world.

5. **The Principle of Successful Adaptation**

    Your ability to adjust successfully to the changing conditions you'll come across is more important than the quality of your plan. Accept what you can't change, change what you can, and watch life unfold. View all roadblocks as opportunities and all obstacles as lessons. Every day is a chance to progress, every hour is a blessing, every moment is vital and every second is precious.

6. **The Principle of Personal Alignment**

    Live out of your imagination, which puts no limitations on your future, rather than from your past, which is history and very limiting. Expressing your true self sets you free and empowers you to create whatever future you can dream for yourself.

7. **The Principle of Love**

    Love others as you love yourself. What you see in the mirror is what you project onto other people. Do this while loving yourself, too. You are the master of your own destiny and can achieve whatever you desire if you have self-love.

8. **The Principle of Trust**

   You cannot respect or trust others if you don't respect or trust yourself first. You are the leader and are also being gently led. The new road ahead of you is clearly marked with trust.

These principles are universal. They are like the sunrise and sunset; always present and always effective. Let them soak in and energise you every dawn.

The best is yet to come

We all know that life is what you make it, that our choices today determine our tomorrows. We know that an attitude of gratitude lifts us spiritually, emotionally, physically and mentally to new levels. We know that unless we are willing to change ourselves, nothing else will change. And, it is with this knowledge that, regardless of age, we can declare with confidence, "The best is yet to come!"

You are who you are, and you have what you have, on purpose and for a purpose. When you live from within that truth, it adds a whole new dimension to your life. The world is changed, one life at a time, and as you allow yourself to change, it has an amazing effect on the people in your circle. You are valuable. You are needed. You are loved. Let your life shine so that others can see the path.

Morning on the earth

Our first family holiday of this year was spent at the beach. My kids sat in my car (a car I completely own), my bills were paid, opportunities were on the horizon and this book was moving from a dream to reality. This holiday was different to all the rest because I had in my life what I'd never had before: space. I no longer had

GOLDEN HOUR AFFIRMATION

I CHOOSE TO RECLAIM
MY IDENTITY AND LIVE
CONSCIOUSLY, ONE MORNING
AT A TIME

#DAWNWARRIOR

the pressures of life consuming me or the feeling that I had lost myself and my identity.

On our last afternoon, there in front of me were my children playing in the sand. The sounds of their laughter carried in the salty air. It didn't matter that it was windy, and it didn't matter that we were hungry... because in that moment all that mattered was life. Life in its most basic, joyful form. Life with moments, with experiences, with family. And as I relished in the sacredness of that moment, the realisation hit me. This was the life I'd written down on butcher's paper only a year earlier, and it had become a reality.

The next morning, watching dawn break over the water, I took a deep inhale and exhale. I breathed in life and breathed out love. A love for my life. Even a love for those years of life when I was so lost and hurting – because they have led me to this exact moment. Do you want to know what the life of a Dawn Warrior really is? It is *right now*. Not the final destination, not the end, but today. Today is your day. Live your best life. Live with hope, joy and courage. Love your kids. Be a friend. And make a start.

Final notes

Take the wisdom of these pages and really sit with it. Remember that insight without inspired action is useless. It's now time to put everything you have read into some serious Dawn Warrior–style action. Dawn Warrior is more than just a morning ritual; it is an entire life design system built from YOUR heart. It is the starting point for your inspired life. And, most importantly, the magic (action-taking) element of your Golden Hour is key to the accomplishment of living your best life. The difference can be summed up with this question: "Do I want to *get* there or *live* there?" You can choose to make your life shine, step-by-step, one morning at a time.

If you ever need clarity or a reminder about the steps in the Dawn Warrior life design system, refer to the following chapter. And if you'd like to receive a list of sources used in the creation of this book – as well as details of inspirational books I recommend – head over to dawnwarrior.com/bookresources. Oh, and don't forget to download your beautiful gift of the *Warrior: One Morning at a Time* print, available at dawnwarrior.com/bookgift!

CHAPTER 17

THE DAWN WARRIOR WAY: A SUMMARY

A life design system built from YOUR heart

The starting point for the creation of your inspired life, one morning at a time

Step 1: Discover your purpose

Get clear on your true needs and desires. Ignore what everyone else is doing and focus on your journey. No one knows what you need more than you do.

Ask yourself:

1. Who am I truly, deeply?
2. What are my top three core values?
3. What lights me up? What are my passions?

Step 2: Live consciously in all areas of your life

Cultivate awareness. The more aware we are, the more possibilities we perceive and the more options we have to live an inspired life.

Ask yourself:

1. What does my ideal life look like? Can I let myself dream of what my ideal day would look like if there were no limitations or consequences?
2. What are my beliefs, goals and strategies across the Five Ps of Life (Physical, Psychological, Partnerships, Parenting and Professional)?
3. What situations am I creating in my life right now that aren't supporting me?

Step 3: Create your life plan & commit to it

Whatever goals you have, large or small, you need to believe in yourself and create a clear path to achieve those goals. You need to take consistent, purposeful action.

Ask yourself:

1. What does my overall life vision look like?
    * Combine the goals from your Five Ps and create a synopsis of your life vision – make it as vivid as possible
2. When I look at my life vision, am I asking enough of myself? Am I willing to pay the price to get it? And will it make me truly happy?

3. What goals have I set to achieve my life vision?
    * Identify your foundational goals – the five or six most important goals that make up your life vision
    * Identify your overriding goal – the most important goal that will drive success in all other areas
    * Identify your annual and quarterly goals
4. What supporting habits will I practise to achieve my inspired life?
    * What daily habits would help to make your life vision AND your annual and quarterly goals a reality? (Pick a few great habits that will create positive change in your life and move you towards your overall life vision.)

Step 4: Harness the dawn

This element is a special way of setting yourself up for success. Designing your mornings gives you the ability to be the best version of yourself and the best role model for your kids. The key to your success will be focusing on the "magic" element of your Golden Hour.

1. What does my Golden Hour look like?
    * Movement – working "out" in a way that is good for you
    * Mindset – working "in" in a way that is good for you
    * Magic – working "on" tasks that are aligned with you
2. In particular, what does my Magic element include?
    * What are you going to work on annually, quarterly and weekly?

* Most importantly, what will be your daily habits or actions?

The process of living The Dawn Warrior Way and creating your most inspired life must be lived and experienced. Wherever you are on your journey, know that you are not alone – trust that I am there with you at dawn, every day.

So take action, tune in to your truth and commit to the steps each and every day.

You've got this, Mama.

IN MEMORIAM

The morning is the best part of the day.
Reg Plath

My connection with my grandfather was one of the game changers in my life. He was my kindred spirit. When I was growing up, it was always fun to be with him. He loved wood-making and we spent hours in his garage sanding, sawing and hammering anything and everything. He had a creative heart, without a doubt. He designed and created many pieces that are still sturdy and beautiful. My kids are sleeping in the cot he made, my mum still writes at the desk he made and my grandma still sits at the phone desk he made.

I have Reg to thank for the fact that I am not afraid to pick up a drill and put a flat pack together or start up the mower. Reg taught me many life lessons that led me to my vision today. He taught me to connect with others and he created lifelong friends this way, forging special bonds with people all over the globe. In fact, as I write this, his friends from Germany are visiting and the people who live where his plane crashed in World War II are coming as well.

Reg taught me to look after others. He always showed my grandmother, Iris, much love and respect. He always opened the car door for her and walked on the pathway closest to the cars to protect her. Reg also taught me how important it is to celebrate life's milestones, big and small. He always made a toast at a family gathering and spoke clearly and intentionally. Toasts are a big thing in our family. Reg taught me the love of travel. We often went on day trips together. He would drive to a place and we would have lunch. He taught me that the journey is the best part in life, not the destination. Reg taught me the art of storytelling. His stories about life were simple, funny and sometimes repetitive as the years went on, but he loved a good ole yarn, that's for sure.

Reg taught me strong family values. But the most profound lesson Reg taught me was the value of every morning. He always started his day with a burst of joyful and unbounded energy. For Reg, the morning was the best part of the day.

Plath the pelican

In my grandfather's final years he spoke fondly about returning as a pelican. He loved the fact that pelicans were social birds, lived a long life and travelled around Australia – my grandfather to a tee. Since his passing, he often appears in the form of a pelican at family occasions – my brother's wedding, my grandmother's birthday and when my sister had her baby. Every time our family sees a pelican, we take a moment and say, "G'day".

IN MEMORIAM

Plath's Coffee House

Reg loved his home and spent many loving hours on its upkeep, painting, maintaining the gardens and giving it the love to stand strong for years to come. My grandfather's house was often referred to as "Plath's Coffee House". It was here that many gatherings took place to fundraise for initiatives at my mum's local school and for youth organisations. My dream is to develop a modern take on Plath's Coffee House, a place where women come together to co-elevate, share knowledge and support one another. This dream fuels my business. It's what drives me to get up every morning and work towards some pretty lofty goals. So lofty is it that I have made a pledge to change 50,000 mums' lives, one morning at a time, by inspiring them to start their day in alignment with life so that they can make a bigger impact for themselves, their family and their community.

Local potter Brooke Clunie custom-made a coffee mug and kindly inscribed Reg's favourite poem on it – "The Clock of Life" by Robert H Smith (I encourage you to look it up online). I read this poem aloud at his funeral, and its words are a loving reminder that all we have is the present, and that we must make the best use of it and live our best life. And I know in my heart that Reg would be proud as stout – his favourite drink – to know that his love for life fuels me every day (as does the coffee) to pursue my dreams of helping others. So, in Reg's true honour, a toast to you: may you live with heart, may you live your now.

My grandfather, Reg – in this photo, he was in his absolute element. He loved to be outdoors, and he had just witnessed my wedding. He radiates with happiness, contentment... and love.

THANKS

I'm deeply grateful to the incredible people in my life who have not only supported me but who have helped me birth Dawn Warrior into the world. So, before the tears start to flow, I want to first acknowledge you, my beautiful reader, for following your heart and picking up this book. Your spirit, your bravery and your willingness to learn, expand and evolve in this lifetime inspires me beyond measure. Stay curious, beautiful soul.

To my divine husband Al – for your unwavering support of my quest to be the fullest version of myself. For being the most kindhearted being with whom to hold hands and walk this lifetime. For your letters of encouragement, whispers of love and kisses of kindness. I love you to Pluto and beyond.

To Austin Reg and Sienna Iris, for gracing this planet with your presence. For choosing me as your mother. For bringing me back to the basics in life and reminding me to play and be present. My heart bursts with love every day for you both.

To my parents, Blair and Helen, for always encouraging me to do what I love and to follow my dreams. Thank you for your unconditional love and support. Dad, your words of wisdom chime loud in my heart. Mum, you're my most treasured teacher and most valued inspiration. You are a beacon of light, always giving to those around you.

To my grandparents, Reg and Iris – my second home. Thank you, Mum [our family's name for Iris], for all the beautiful stories shared over a cuppa and for the genuine love and care you give. Reg, I miss you every single day and can't thank you enough for the imprint you have left deep in my heart.

To my in-laws Brian, June and Robyn, not only for raising Al, but for expanding my heart and welcoming me into yours so openly.

To my beautiful siblings Aaron and Corene, for loving me at my worst and best, and for showing up for me. I'm grateful that we share our timeline of life together. And your incredible partners Darcy and Ali, thank you for your friendship and unconditional love.

It's with thanks to all my dear friends, near and far, for being the sunshine in my life.

To all my teachers and mentors, thank you for your soulful guidance, heartfelt interest and reminding me of the truth within.

To Sally Wolfe for being the backbone of my visions and dreams. Your expertise, insights and wisdom have been invaluable to this process... thank you.

To Joanne Newell and Amy De Wolfe, for your support with this book. You played an instrumental role in shaping every aspect of it, from the content to the cover design to the marketing strategy.

To the thought leaders for inspiring us all to live our self-expressed lives.

THANKS

A big shout out to the modern mamas. Thank you for trusting me to guide you towards reaching your goals. Your accomplishments become my success stories and I continue to feel so proud of you.

ABOUT TARA

After experiencing the devastation of miscarriage and the emotional and physical upheaval of IVF, Tara Hegerty is now the mother of two beautiful young children.

Like so many other women, Tara experienced a huge identity shift when she became a mother. She felt overwhelmed, anxious, inadequate and guilty, and wondered if she would ever feel truly happy and connected to her soul.

While in the depths of despair, Tara began listening to the tug of her heart, and was inspired by her grandfather's love of finding the joy in each new morning.

She also implemented powerful personal growth tools that have transformed her life. Through her one-on-one and group-based mentoring, she now teaches mothers how to live their most inspired lives. She helps them to see that motherhood is a life passage that can be utterly, positively transformational.

Tara lives in Brisbane with her husband Al and children Austin and Sienna. When not exploring the great outdoors (including sashaying down ski slopes), she loves being with family and friends, chatting with Al over a bonfire and a G&T, and devouring books about spiritual adventures.

To discover more about Tara and how she can help you to become an empowered mama, head to dawnwarrior.com.

THE DAWN WARRIOR WAY

MAMA, IT'S TIME TO PUT YOURSELF FIRST.
Not just so that you can be a better mother, but because you are a *human being* and you deserve it!

Would you like to know what it's like to feel good
(like, truly good – possibly for the first time in your life),
be a great mum and pursue your dreams?

Let yourself receive the inspiration and support you've been craving.
Come and join me, and other like-minded mamas, in

THE DAWN WARRIOR WAY PROGRAM.

Intrigued? Listen to the pull of your soul, and head here to discover more:

dawnwarrior.com/dawnwarriorway

REVIEW REQUEST

Dear Reader

If my book has struck a chord with you, I would love to hear what it was that resonated with you.

I would really appreciate it if you could share your thoughts by leaving a review.

To do this, simply go to the review section on the Amazon page for *Dawn Warrior*. Click on the big button that says "Write a customer review" and enter your star rating and written review.

Thank you so much...

Tara xx

PS I would love to see you enjoying this book – please share a photo of yourself with the book on Facebook, and tag me by using @dawnwarrior.

www.ingramcontent.com/pod-product-compliance
Lightning Source LLC
Chambersburg PA
CBHW021949290426
44108CB00012B/1004